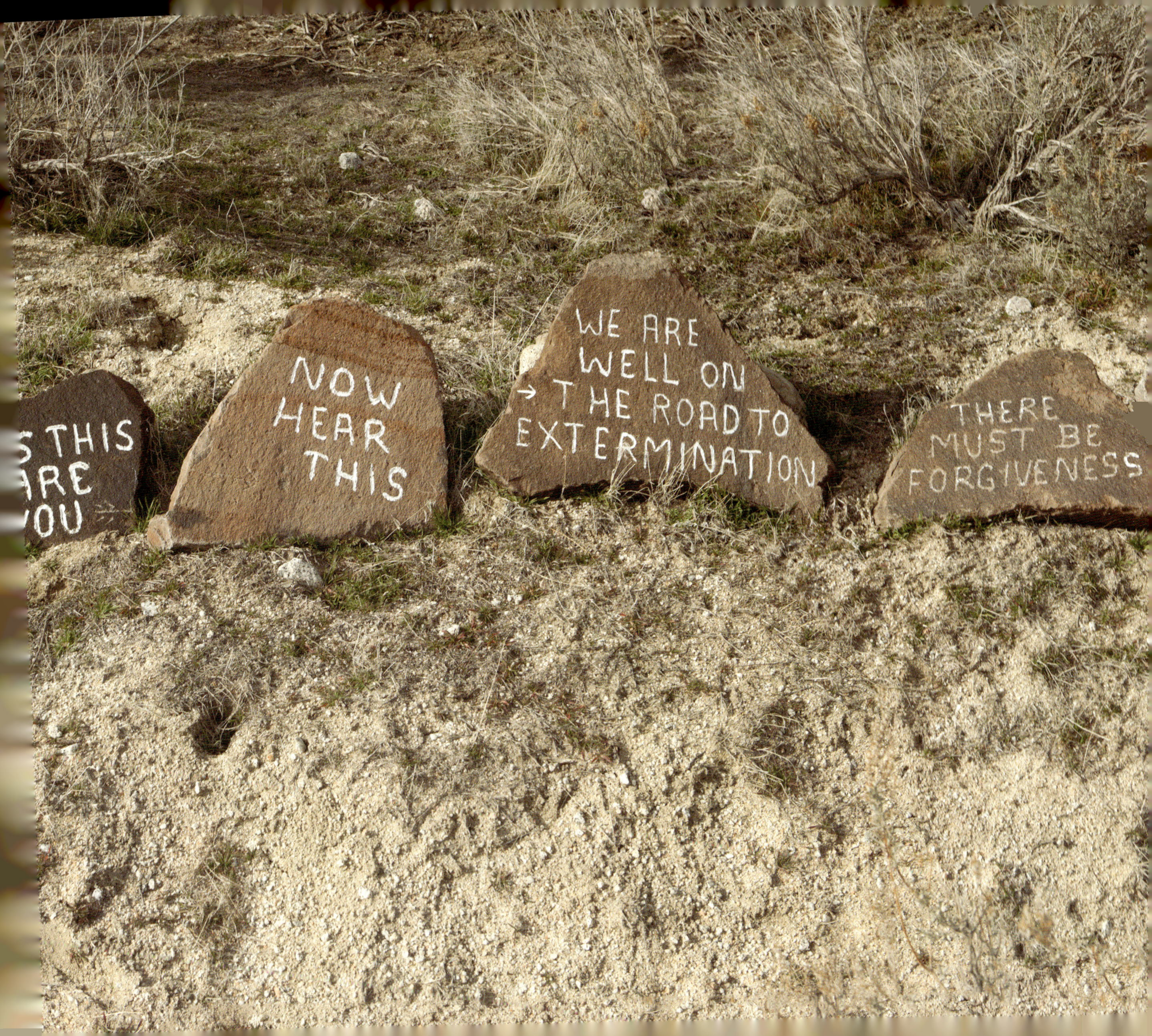
THIS
NOW HEAR THIS
WE ARE WELL ON THE ROAD TO EXTERMINATION
THERE MUST BE FORGIVENESS

DOOBY LANE

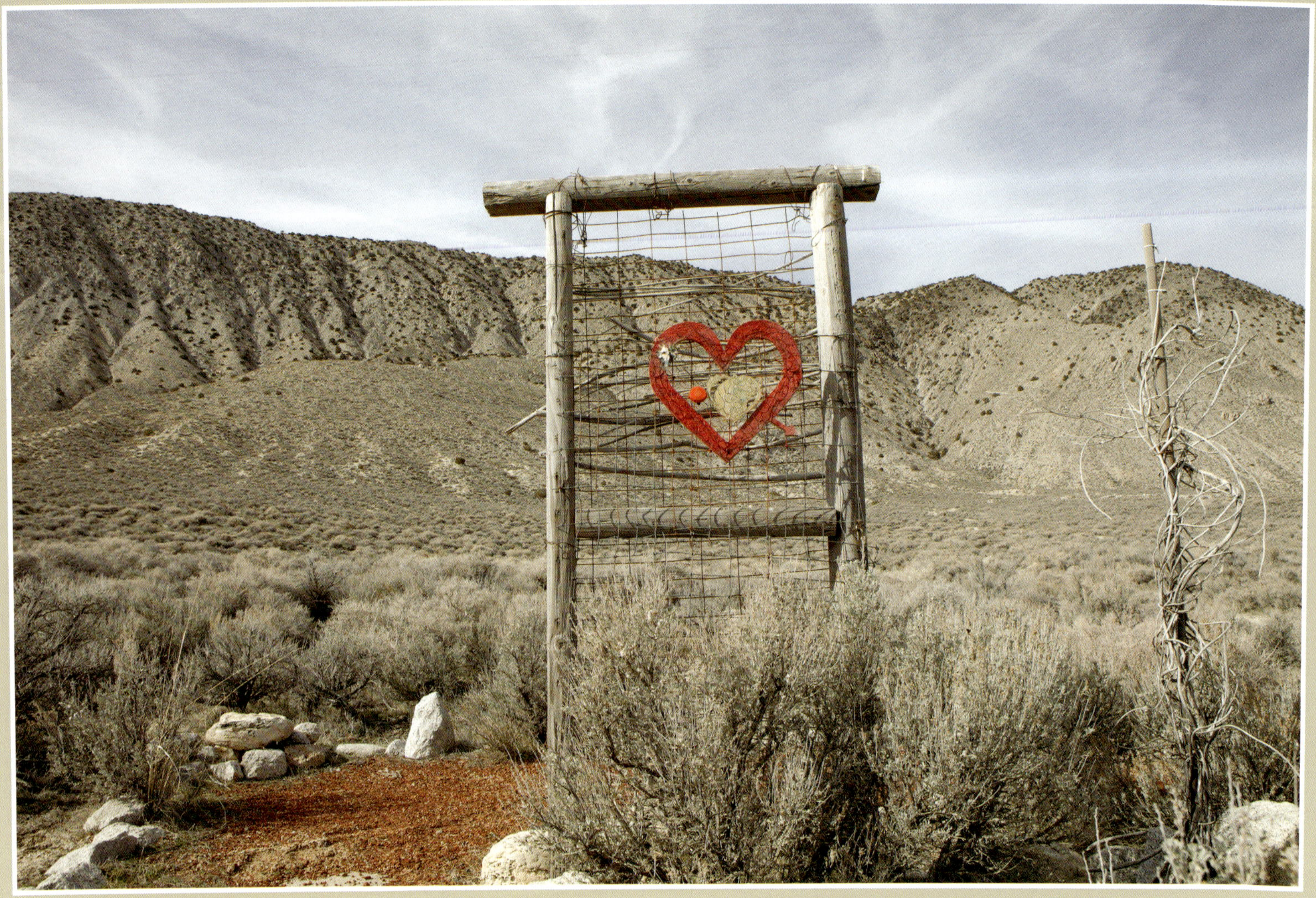

DOOBY LANE

ALSO KNOWN
AS *Guru Road*,
A TESTAMENT
INSCRIBED
IN STONE
TABLETS

PHOTOGRAPHS BY Peter Goin
FIELD NOTES BY Gary Snyder

COUNTERPOINT
BERKELEY

Library of Congress Cataloging-in-Publication Data Is Available

ISBN 978-1-61902-790-9

COUNTERPOINT
2560 Ninth Street, Suite 318
Berkeley, CA 94710
www.counterpointpress.com

Printed in Canada
Distributed by Publishers Group West

10 9 8 7 6 5 4 3 2 1

Contents

Preface

BY GARY SNYDER

Almost twenty years ago now Carole and I were camping on the edges of the Black Rock Desert playa (my old haunt) exploring the bajada slopes off the Granite Range that led down to it, the back roads and side roads, before just heading out into the vast flats.

Just a few miles north of the tiny settlement of Gerlach we noticed the dirt road off the paved road and tried it. It was Guru Road, Dooby Lane. And so we had discovered this remarkable text of life and spirit. What was there that day is recorded here.

On a later trip I ran into the maker, DeWayne Williams, even as he was working on a new installation. He had a little house in Gerlach, had been born on a ranch not far away, and had spent some years in the farther world. Then retired, with cancer, he was making his final life statement—with what flair and freedom! The sixties surely had happened just so this man would know he could leave his thoughts on life and love and friendship on stone and out in the open. His cancer was eased by the dooby, and he was also trying "a mushroom from China" that gave him some hope, but in any case his spirit was good.

The next time I went out there he was gone. We circled our wagons and made camp way out on the playa, near the almost gone wrecked Plymouth car we called "Plymouth Wreck," and I thought long of DeWayne and what he left behind. Later John Balkwill and Peter Goin at the University in Reno got into it and together with Peter's students made the 1996 accordion-fold book (refer to page 86). The road has changed over time. DeWayne made changes year by year 'til he died, and then the Gerlach folks both kept it up and added a few notes of their own. It sits alone and vulnerable in the big space, but it is also known and loved. A dusty book, a text, a story, out there for as long as the world lets it be. Now with *Dooby Lane* updated and expanded containing 108 photographs without which no one would know how it really looks, Dooby Lane can be seen from far away.

Carole's gone now also, and the Black Rock playa too well known—the BLM has inventoried it and the art and I.T. worlds appropriated it. Just another drip of dew on old Lake Lahontan though—his words may disappear, but Dooby's teachings are for all time and will keep on echoing in the sagebrush and juniper down the line.

"The Best Things in Life are Not Things."

30.IX.07

Field Notes

BY GARY SNYDER

Dooby Lane, just north of Gerlach.
A testament inscribed in stone tablets.

Gerlach, a town of 150, 100 miles from Reno, "Where the Pavement Ends and the West Begins," at the edge of the Black Rock Desert (to the east) and the High Rock Canyon country to the north. Continuing out of Gerlach, past Bruno's Gas, Bruno's Motel, Bruno's Bar and Bruno's Café, taking the fork toward Vya, a mile or so.

An improbable green official-looking metal sign, Guru Rd., that you might easily miss, and a wooden sign low to the ground that says "Dooby Lane." Up through the sagebrush and onto a worn-in track.

Soon, a bulldozed-out leveled area to the left, where several cars could park. A smooth gray rock standing vertical on the top of the bank above — 18" high and the same wide, clean letter engraved into it, it says

A Good Place to Make Love.

Just a bit down the road, a series of inscribed rocks standing with their flat faces toward the dirt road, clear sans-serif Romans scratched through desert varnish,

A light gray rock: Special People
Next rock, brown: V.I.P. Bob Gooch
Four smaller rocks in a row: Maybe We All Should
Look So
Good with an arrow
As Marian Gooch

Carole Minto   Gary and Trudy Minto

& on, for hundreds of feet, series after series of standing rocks inscribed with names and comments and religio-political insights, along the dirt-road desert lane running parallel to the paved highway. Beyond that the playa. Above and behind Dooby Lane are the lower slopes of the Granite Range, with mostly sage, and a few juniper on the flanks.

Continuing, Doug and Robin Watt on a rock
Tom Cat and Diana Rios   Dale Doedle   Pot of Gold
Ardie Johns   Tim and Vicki Williams
Mitch and Connie Ugalde
I am the Greatest, Ask Grandma   Michael Ugalde   Stuart
Welcome Aboard   Dan and Dinky Wardle
Owen and Carmen Wardle
Neat Folks   Jean and Anita Reap
David, Toot on the Road Again
People Who Are Famous   Amy Lou Weldon
Miss Personality   Torri Conley
Stars on the Horizon   Becky Green   Vanessa Dinekan
Russell Minto
We Are the Future   Susan Rios   Cecil Courtney   Ashley Mott
'88 . . . Dylan Watt   Buddy Minto   Michael Ugalde
Eirk Henjum
People who Care   Mary Minn . . .   Dan Devony
Patsy Stimac

No Words, Just Action
Brian Covey   The Word Is Impulse

All, with lists of names after, each name or pairs of names on a separate standing stone.
Fifty feet and another group:

People Who Live and Let Live   Al Linda and Jim Boegle
Keeping the West Alive   Jackie Sid, and Kelly Lyles

Eight more feet open, and then
Fred Chez Has the Beef
And I Have Fred
Jo Chez

A rock standing by itself, a nice tall one:
Nothing So Small That You Can't Cut It In Half,
Nothing So Large That You Can't Double It

Fifty more feet along.   Yaqui Joe Garcia One of the Best
One in a million.   Fred Schoenfeld
A blank rock facing the road, all set up.
Best in the West . . .   Beth Williams
85,   Mr. Dylan DeWayne Watt

Standing by itself: Gourmet Cook   Leonard Williams
Desert Diamonds   Joanne and Vanessa Dunnigan
By itself: Never too Busy to Talk to a Friend   Joe Selmi
A Ray of Sunshine *(one rock)* Sharon Duren
Kipping Vesey Is My Name and Poetry Is My Game
My Fans   Al and Lucille Evans   Philly Williams
Back a ways from the road stood a twisty juniper trunk with a rock hanging from a string from a limb, with stone inscription below:
If Rock Above Is Moving, Wind's Blowing
Wet It's Raining White It's Snowing   Gerlach Weather Station

A big natural rock says just DeWayne

Jeff and Ricka Very Sincere
Champion Lover, Fighter, and Wild Bull Rider Dale Bocgle
Mink, Gold, Diamonds Ardie Johns
Doo?bie? *with a reverse crescent, a dot inside the crescent, lines shooting out around it, all in a rather fancy script.*

Next to God Is Woman I Know I Have This One Right
Don't You Forget It *the last rock says* Ask Nancy

Variety Is the Real Spice of Life Jan Hendershot
Another series.

It's Hazard to Be Born Poor
The Rebel Dave Clapper
I Will Always Return Lloyd Custer Mosley
One Big Tomahawk
A sort of tomahawk-looking rock.

The Best Things in Life Are Not Things
A Loss Is a Win Just Knowing You Have One Hundred Friends
Thanks For Your Support Love Ya Doobie

Another Group.
Waste Not Want Not Birds Please Shit on the Rock.
This Painting Is By the Birds *back of that a tall single-rock-pile chorten, thirteen rocks high.*

What Goes Around Comes Around China Will Rise Again

Who Keeps Gerlach Smart Dave Green That Is Who
Knowledge Is The Key To Power Go For It

What a Brain Used to Look Like Now *a drawing of a brain, with its lobes.* What a Brain Looks Like Now *a drawing of a football. All this is done on flat faces of standing rocks . . .*

Here is a teepee frame set up, full size with poles & some antlers hanging down within, between the poles.

This Structure for Rent or Lease, Call 557-2296
Come to the Wigwam   Fernley Nevada   Mary and Moe

A Word From Space   Never Say Die   Don't Panic
Time is of the Essence, Let's Use it Wisely
It's Your Trip   Aids Will Unite us All

The More You See the Better You Like   Terry Weldon

The World Needs More People Like You   Annette Marshall
Do Blondes Have More Fun   Rand and Kay Henjum
A Star Is Born   Eric Henjum

A big rock with an upside-down washbasin on the top of it.

People You Should Meet   Bev and Arlie Osborn
Shelley McKnight   Smiley   Mr. Music
Randy McKnight   Kool Rise

I Call the Shots   Sunny Schatz   1985 Linda Campbell
Rest Your Dog Here   *next to a post stuck in the ground.*
A broken heart with an arrow through it, all by itself on a rock.

John and Cindy Carter   You Must Have Something to Do
Someone to Love, Something to Believe In
Believe In Yourself   And Be Sure
That's on four rocks.

Filmed in Gerlach   Far From Home   Starring Drew Barrymore
Four cow skulls with painted horns hanging on a dead twisted juniper. Inscription: Tree Planted By Doobie
    Please Don't Pick the Fruit

Clifford Williams   Burt Eckharty   Ruby Janus
Written vertically.

A ways on, Gateway to life Eternal *and nice little garden gate of wood, with vertical pickets, setting there in the nowhere of the desert, the gate closed, white hinges & through that a path leading back to a stone that says:* You Must Have a guide Guru There Will Be No Work in Heaven
No One Is Going to Screw It Up How Do You Know Are You Sure Are You Really Sure

A pair of rocks. I Love My Critics S. Tyler, Carson City Suzie Says DOOBIE THE GURU OF GERLACH
Don't Worry Be Happy   You Must Force Yourself   Start Today

"A Rich Man Has the Same Chance of Entering Heaven as a Camel Going thru the Eye of a Needle"
Check this Out

The Ultra Rich
  Herbert Armstrong   Jerry Falwell Billy Graham Jim Bakker Jim Swaggert

As I Understand   God Loves Us All
Not Because of What We Are
Do You Believe That the Blind Are Leading the Blind
Here are two forks set in the ground, painted around the crotches so they look like two boys wearing colored shorts, maybe one's supposed to be a girl, the crotch looks rather cunt-like, No Tools, no discrimination, no sex *it says.*
They both have little belly-buttons stuck on.

Keeping Our History Alive   Ken and Irene McCurdy   Patsy

Dedicated People   Dale, Gail, and Renee Carter   Rand Henjum

Good Neighbors   Ed and Ann Mayer
Honesty First   Jim Spoo for Governor   Most Important Man

Some whiskey and beer bottles lined up lying on the ground,
The Lost

Never Forget you're Very Important *names I can't read*   Visit
I Would Rather Be in Gerlach   Frank Davis
A Very Good Citizen   Skipper Douglas
Lady Slippers Says   Marie Morissey a Total Friend
Hamm's Champion Drew Douglas   A lot of PP
To Have a Friend You Must Be a Friend

Politicians *And just below this rock is a pile of dried cowshit.*
After Taxes Picked Clean
and on the sand vertebrae, ribs, a cow?
Ralph Nader for President He Is Working for Us
Clean Air Clean   Bob and Edna Spoo   High Integrity
Good Morals   Great Friends

The Men That Can Do It Ned Waldmar
Those who Dare Beware Bill Flippo Is Everywhere

Workaholic Bill Green Very Lovely Lady Mudge Green
I Have a Secret to Stay Young Lena Luccjesi
Plus Health Wealthy

Sweetheart of Gerlach Empire   Jane Anderson
Very Pretty Things to See in Gerlach Crystal Carter
Chrissie Stimac Beauty and Brain

Tony Diebold Great White Trapper Ardine Diebol

Are You Ready For Tonnie's Last Act Fire in the Sky
Mushroom Cloud I Was Right, Jane Wyman
Lots of bones spread on the ground below these stones.
Let's Share the Wealth *then here's some bones on a rock.*
Last of Black Rock   Big Jim and Lois Watt

Why Take More Than You Need   Take a Break *by a big log*
No One on This Earth is Greater Than You
Amen To That   Halleluja

Then two toilet bowls
The Equalizers

What Would the World Have Been Like Without You In It

The Outstanding People   Bud and Bard Conley
1984 Sweet Judie and Steve Conley

Love of Money Saps the Goodness from Man *says a rock.*

And here's another cairn on the right, nicely put together.
Crème de la Crème Nancy Iveson
Fine Fellow Cecil Courtney
The Queen Bee Skeky Courtney
I Am the One Cecil Courtney
Never Underestimate the Powers of a Woman Jeannie Casey
Doobie's Commandments

Stomp Out Greed

Keep Smiling

Think Health

Wipe Out Envy

Never Assume

Believe Only What Can Be Proved.

I Have a Dream. Perfect Wife and Mother Evelyn Williams.

Make the Whole World Smile *A rock I can't read*
Home of Edward Meese and it looks like a woodrat nest
And we go out through a very elegantly done cairn, Gerlach Oil
Supply Depot *A funny little model oil derrick about 10 feet high*

Life is Nothing but a Big Joke
Kick Back and Watch the Show—Guru

Opinions Are Lie . . . . ? Everyone Has One
And They All Stink

A few hundred yards of nothing alongside the road. And then another one of these improbable cairns . . . rock balanced on rock.

(This is just two tracks in the sagebrush and rabbitbrush.)

The Lost Buffalo *A rock standing by itself. Another little cairn on the right. Were going out through a little gap with cairns on each side of it, right up near the paved road, and three cairns across the paved road, and this is end of the inscribed rocks on Dooby Lane; the dirt road leading onto the vast playa of the Black Rock Desert is just beyond.*

Recorded together with Carole on 21 October 1988 in the morning. Later we went into Bruno's Café and asked the young waitress what about Dooby Lane. Never heard of it, she said. Older waitress came by said, "Yeah, DeWayne Williams, Robin Watts's father."

In this climate, these stones will be legible for several thousand years.

We found the desert dirt track known as Guru Avenue or Dooby Lane by chance. I walked through the unfolding tale of a community, and the wise and funny tablets of philosophy and advice, with amazement and delight. I was moved to record it on the spot. And later met DeWayne the maker on the very road, doing another installation. It was my luck to get to be his scribe.

Gary Snyder
Summer 1996

Photo Gallery

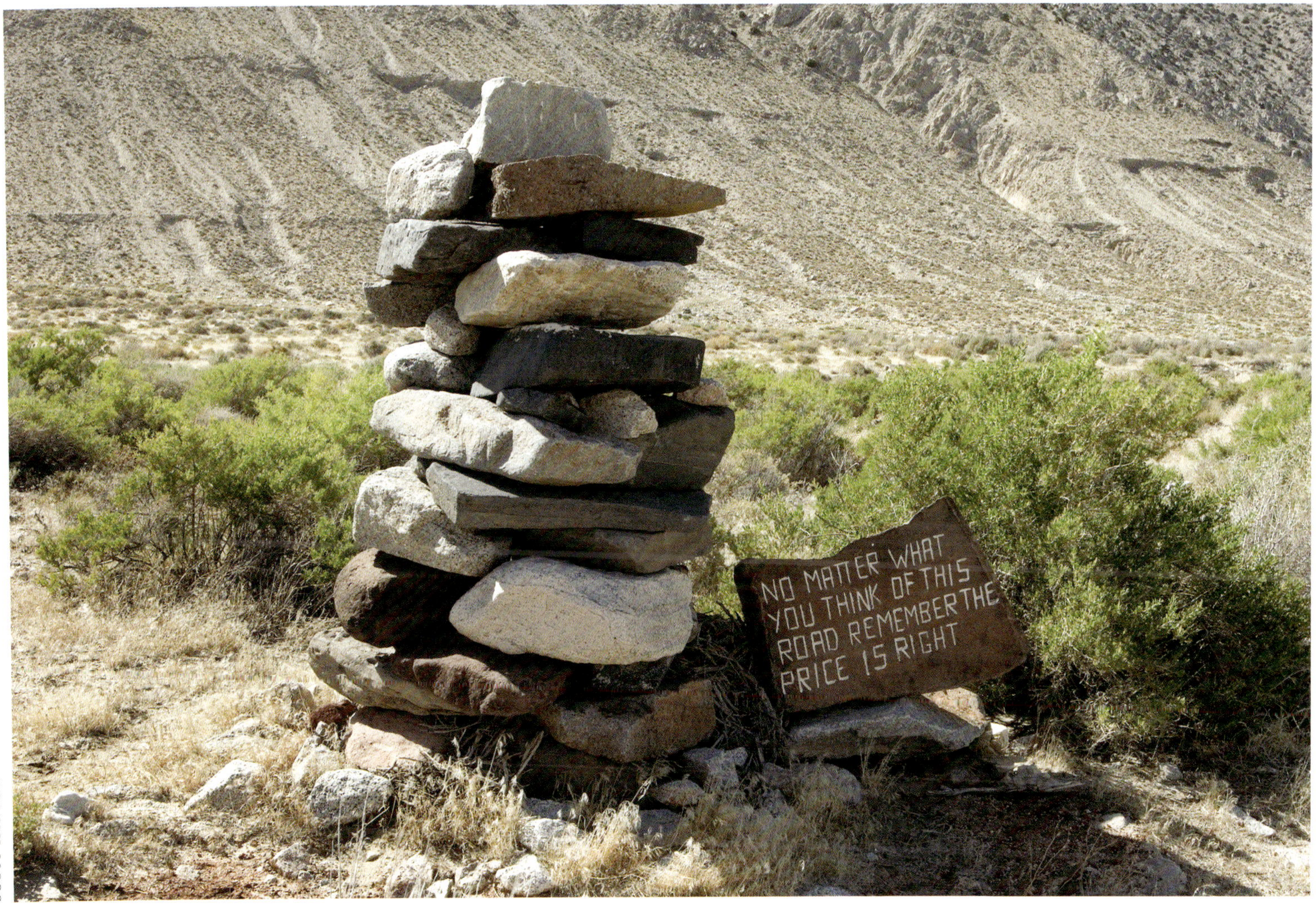
NO MATTER WHAT
YOU THINK OF THIS
ROAD REMEMBER THE
PRICE IS RIGHT

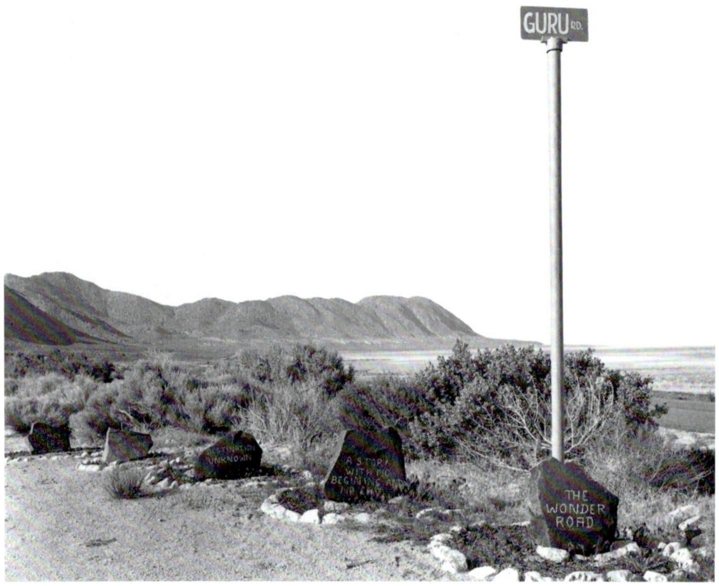

Irene Kung

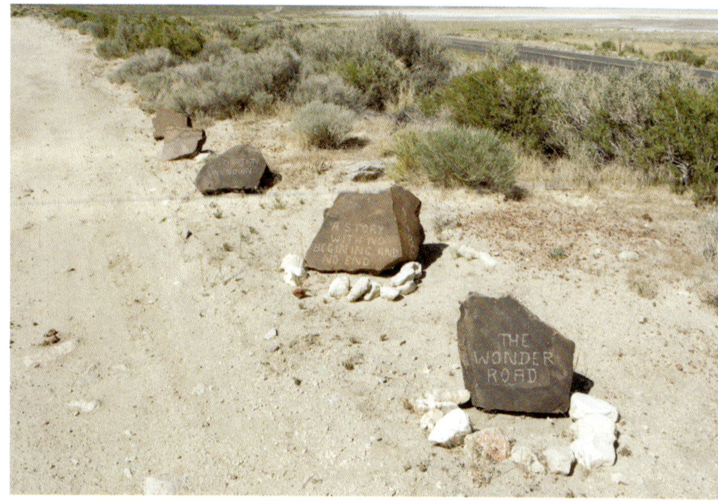

Scott Hinton

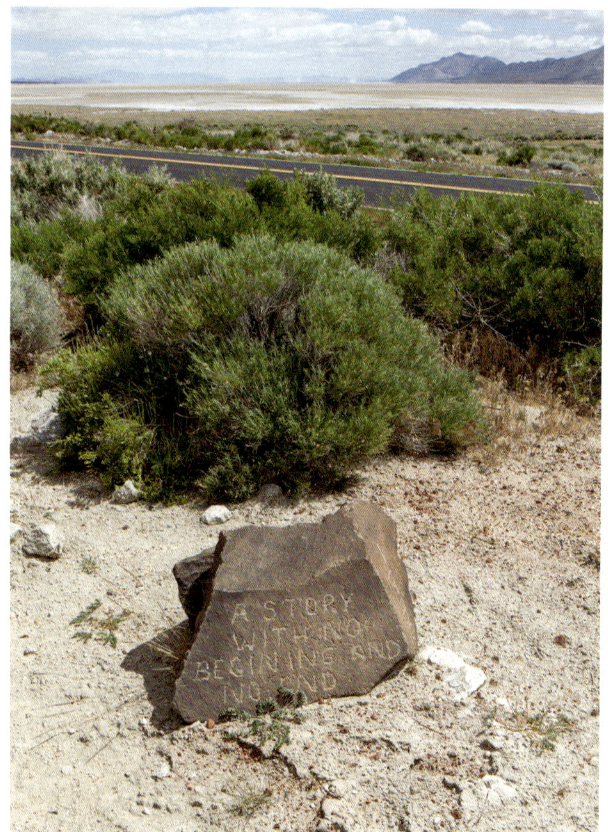

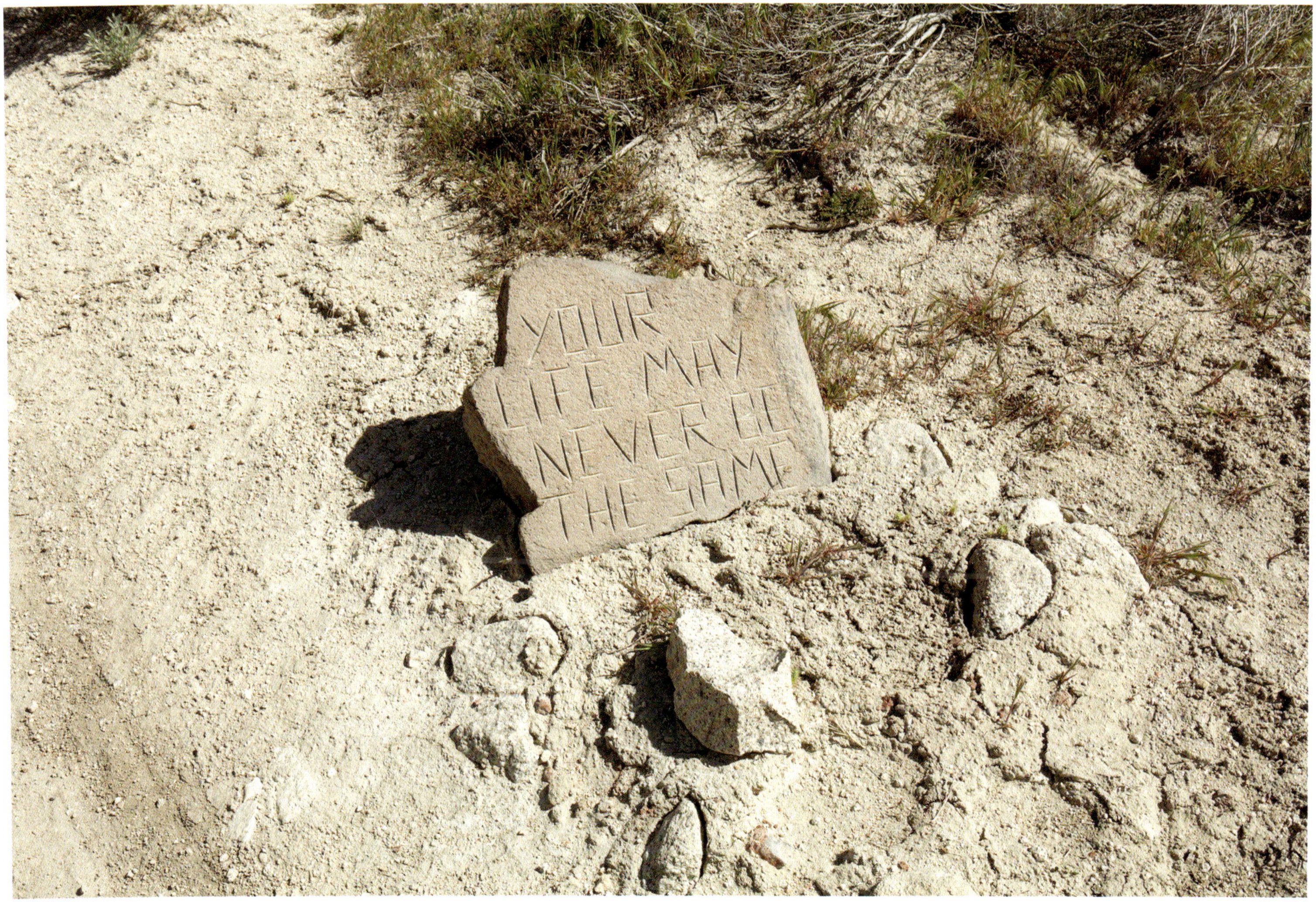
YOUR
LIFE MAY
NEVER BE
THE SAME

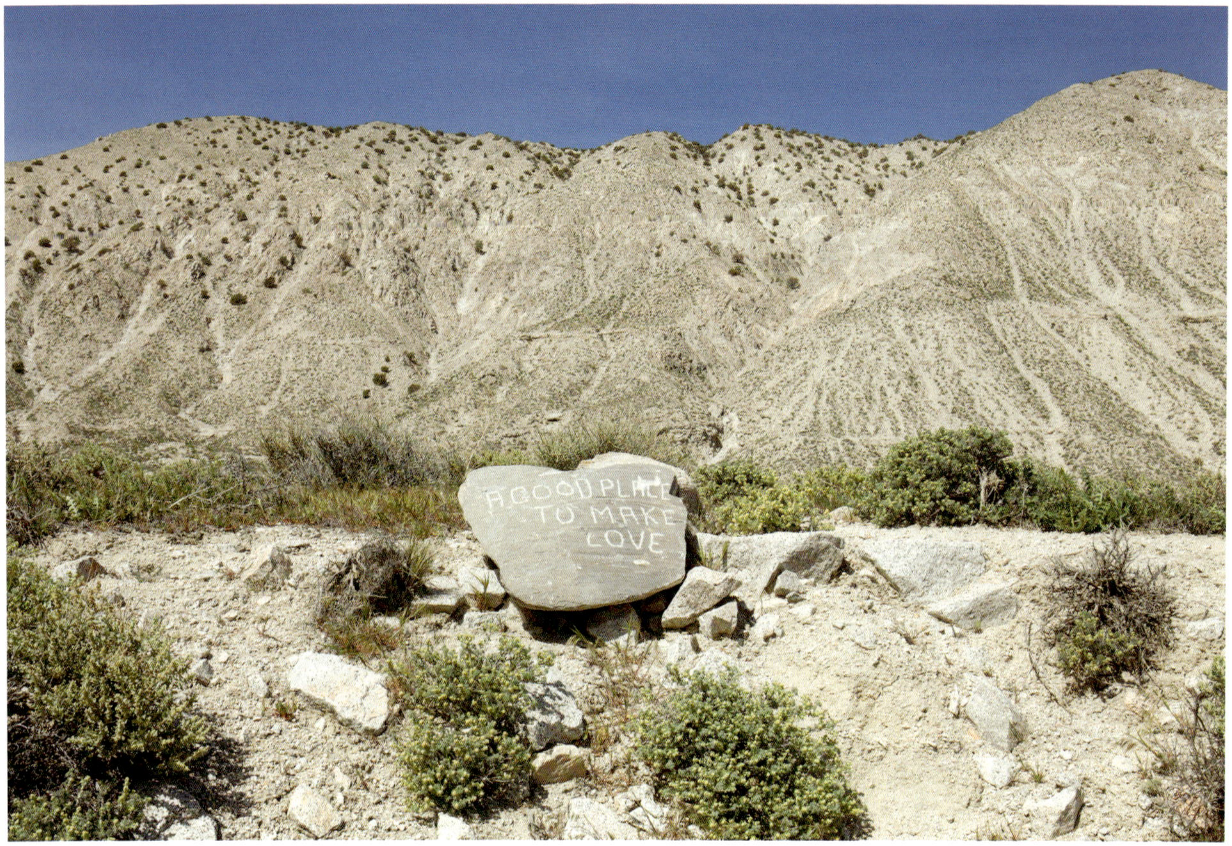
A GOOD PLACE
TO MAKE
LOVE

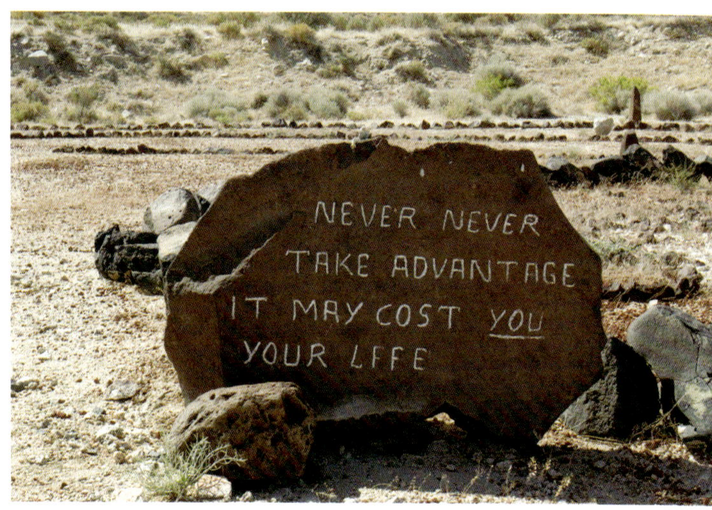
NEVER NEVER
TAKE ADVANTAGE
IT MAY COST YOU
YOUR LIFE

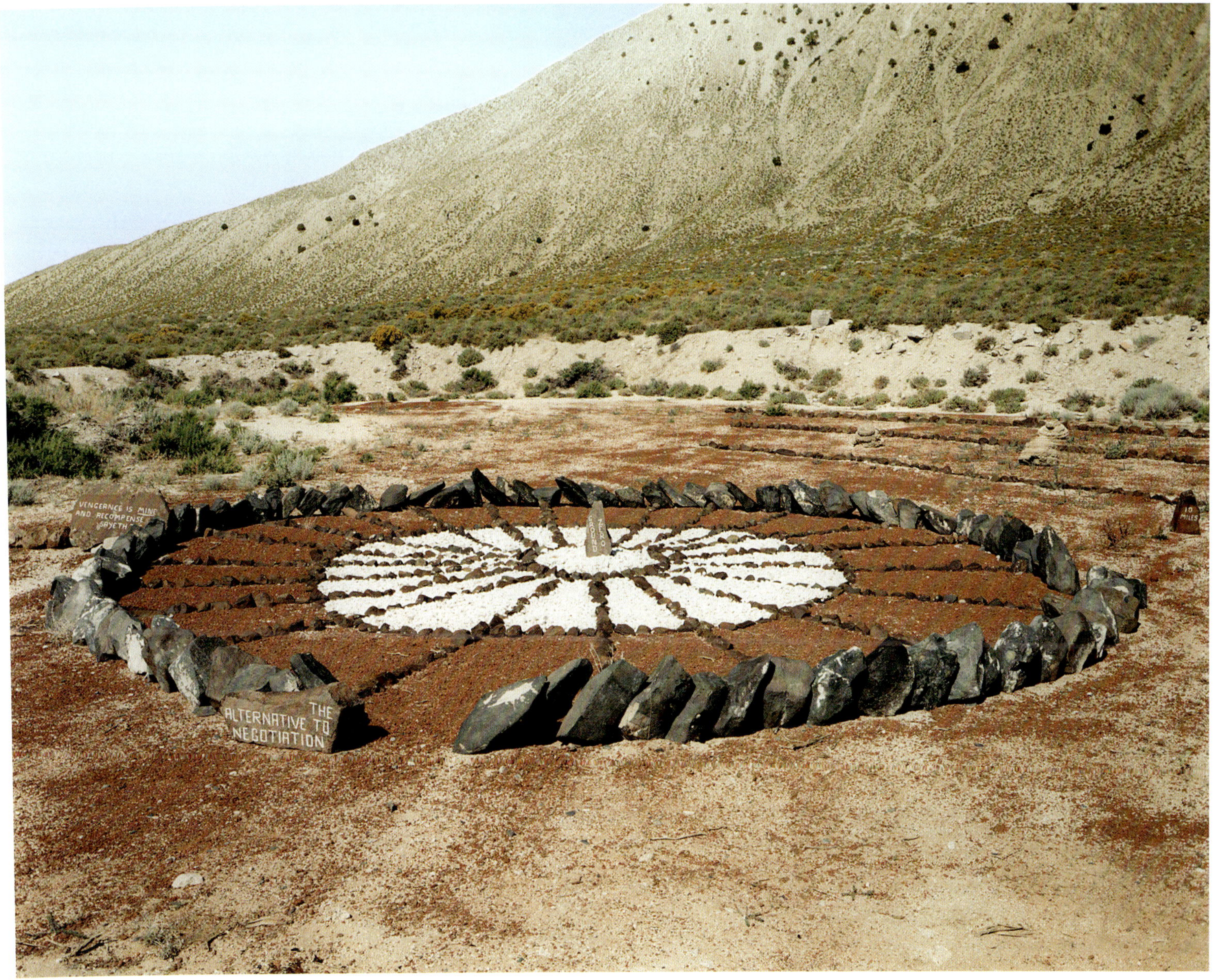
VENGERNCE IS MINE
AND RECOMPENSE
SAYETH
GROUND ZERO
10 MILES
THE
ALTERNATIVE TO
NEGOTIATION

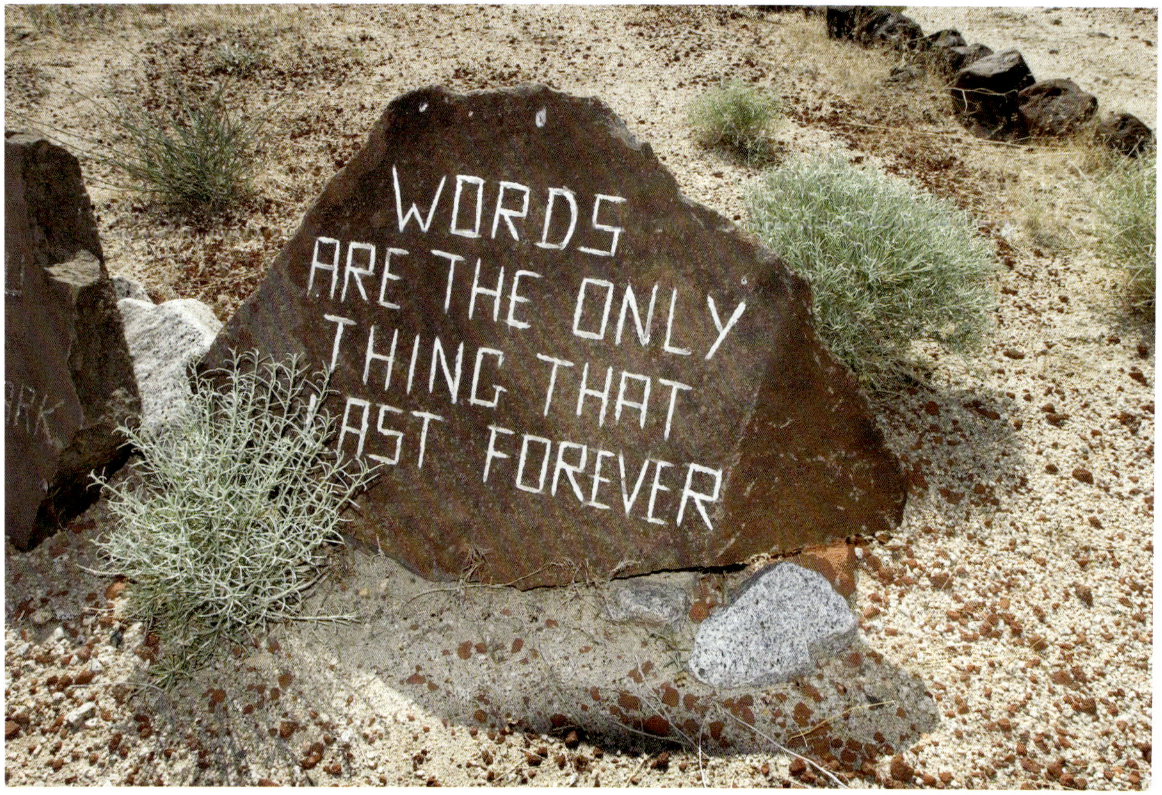
WORDS
ARE THE ONLY
THING THAT
AST FOREVER

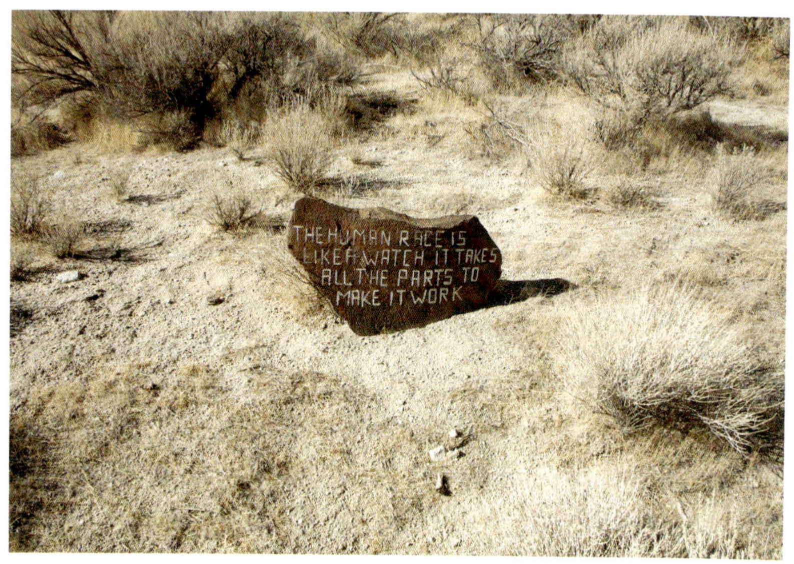
THE HUMAN RACE IS
LIKE A WATCH IT TAKES
ALL THE PARTS TO
MAKE IT WORK

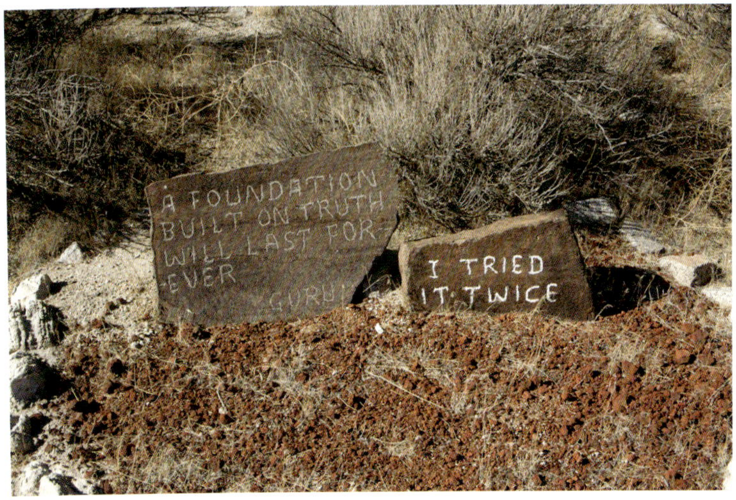
A FOUNDATION
BUILT ON TRUTH
WILL LAST FOR-
EVER
GURU
I TRIED
IT TWICE

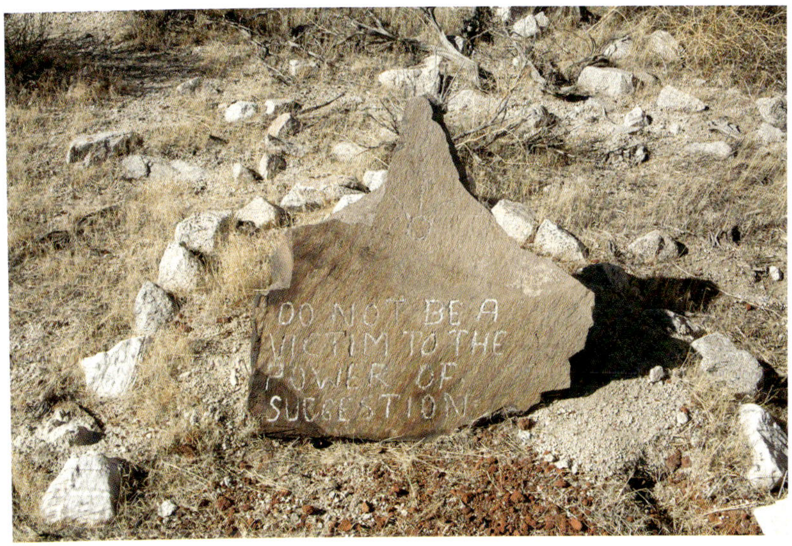
DO NOT BE A
VICTIM TO THE
POWER OF
SUGGESTION

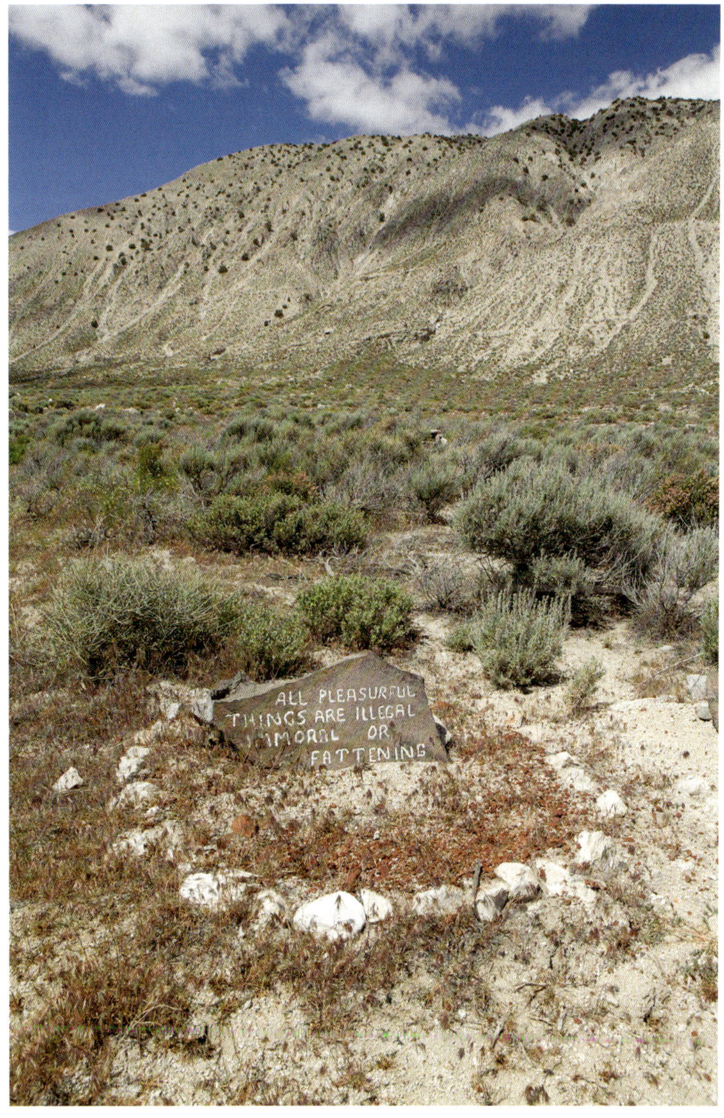
ALL PLEASURFUL
THINGS ARE ILLEGAL
OR
FATTENING

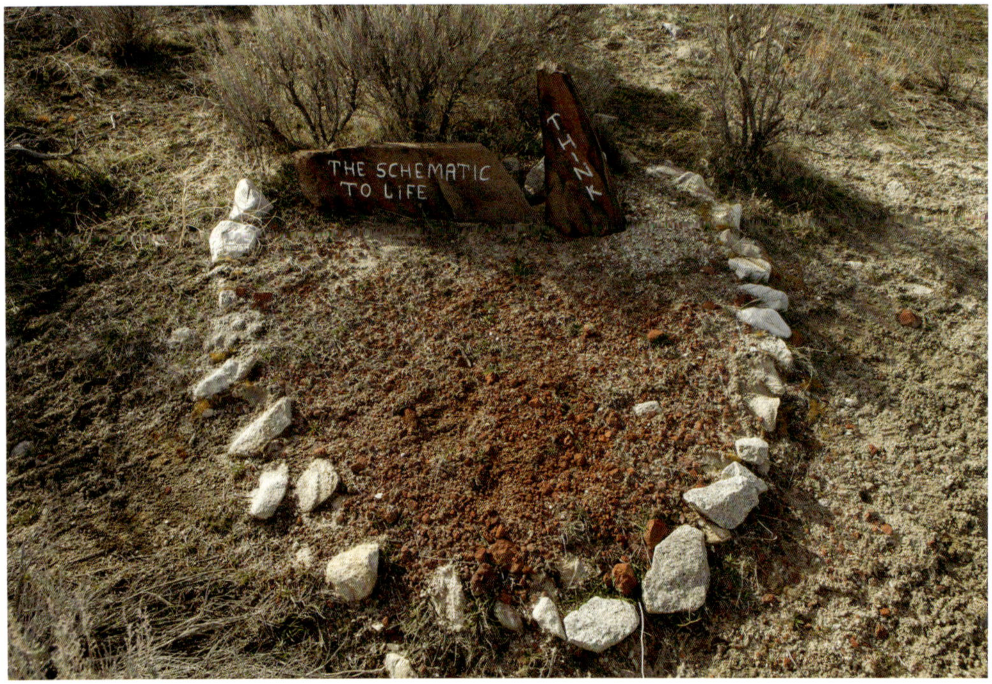
THE SCHEMATIC
TO LIFE
THINK

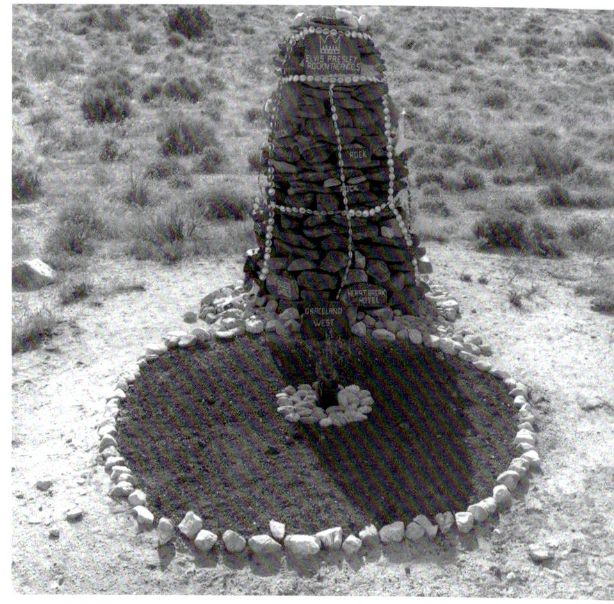
ELVIS PRESLEY
ROCK N THE ANGELS
ROCK
ROCK
HEARTBREAK
HOTEL
GRACELAND
WEST

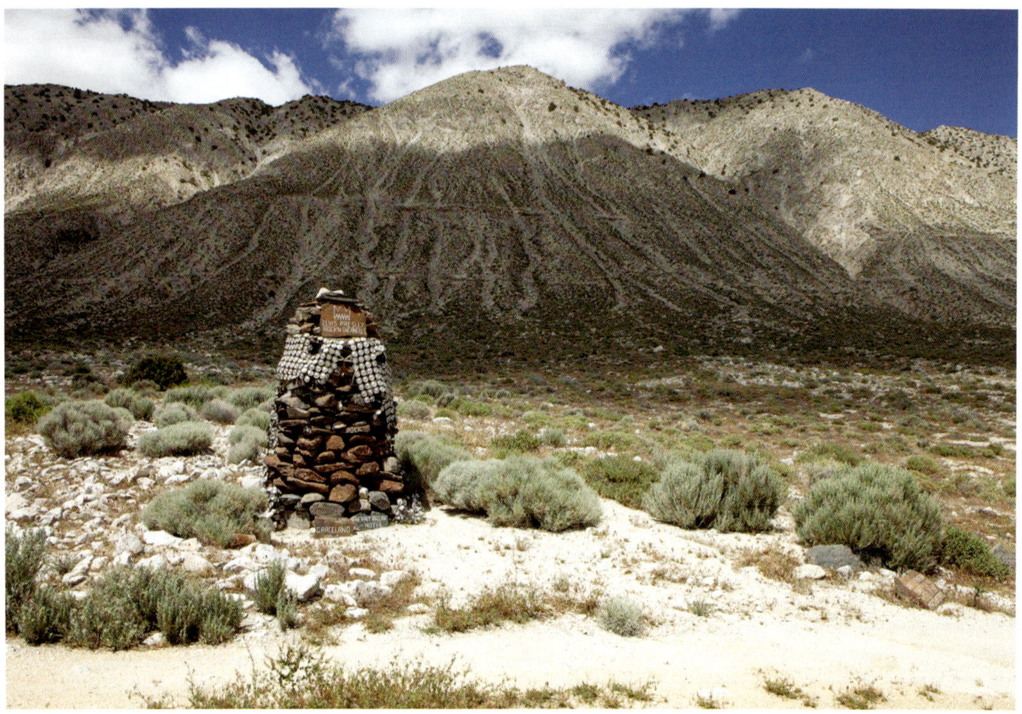

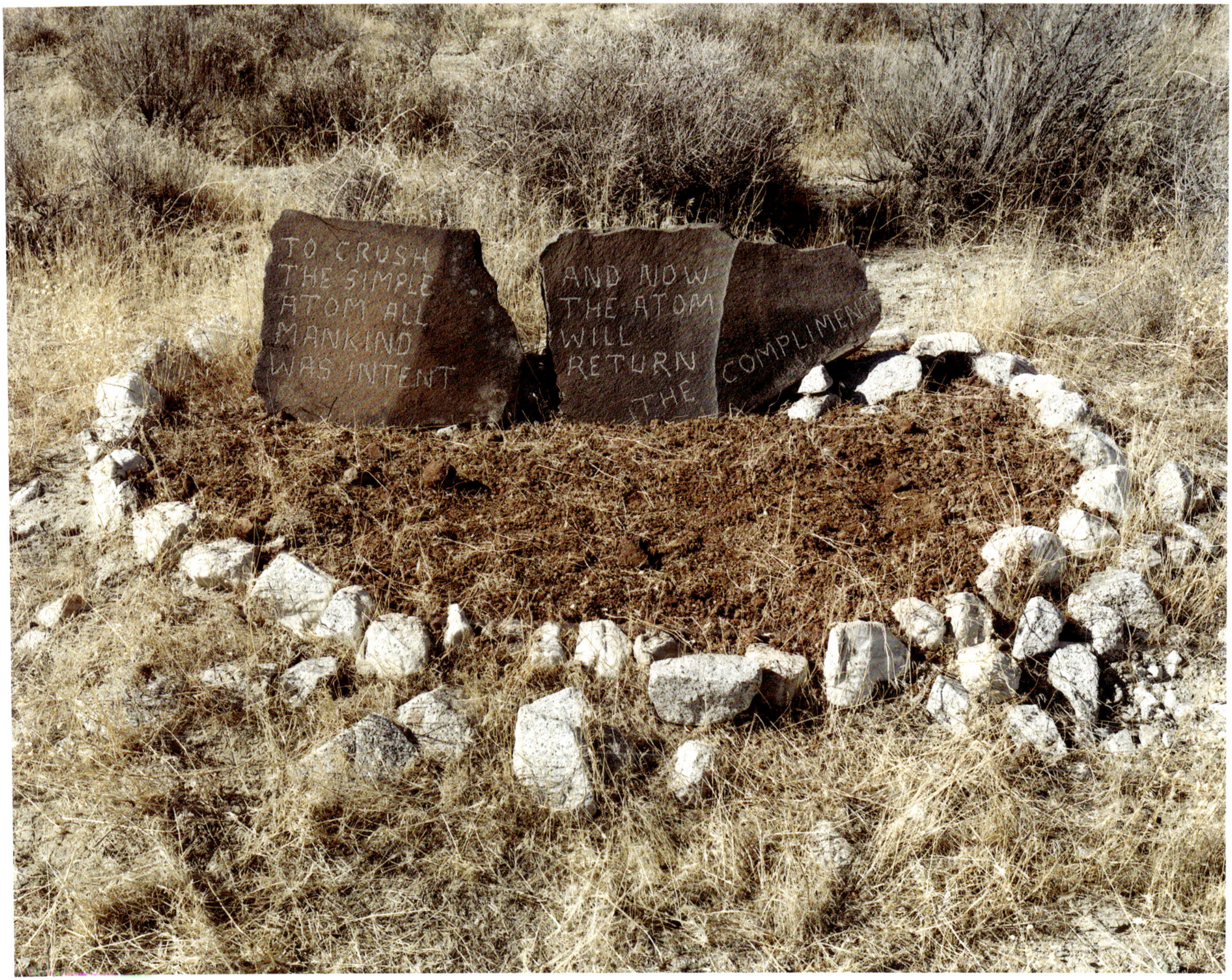
TO CRUSH
THE SIMPLE
ATOM ALL
MANKIND
WAS INTENT
AND NOW
THE ATOM
WILL
RETURN
THE
COMPLIMENT

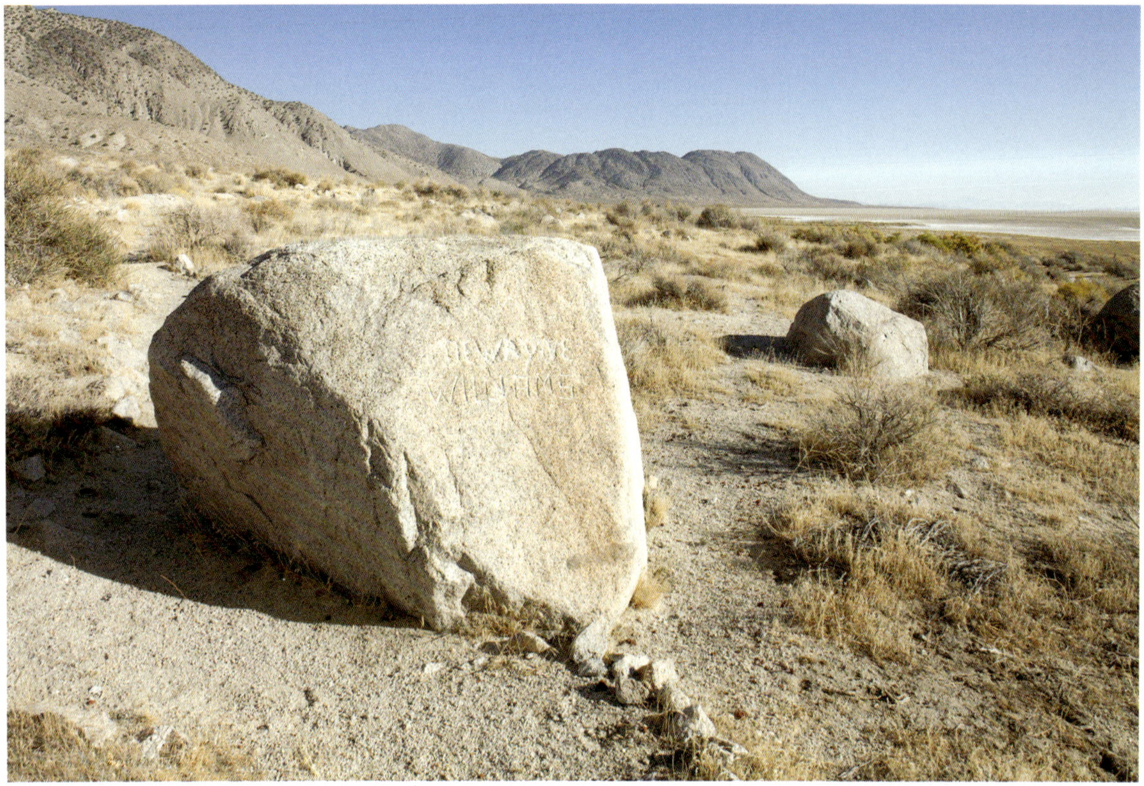

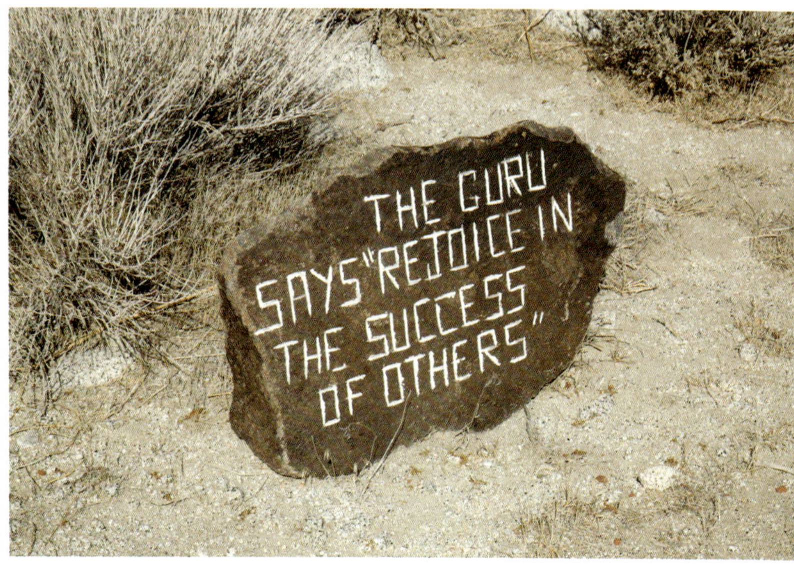
THE GURU
SAYS "REJOICE IN
THE SUCCESS
OF OTHERS"

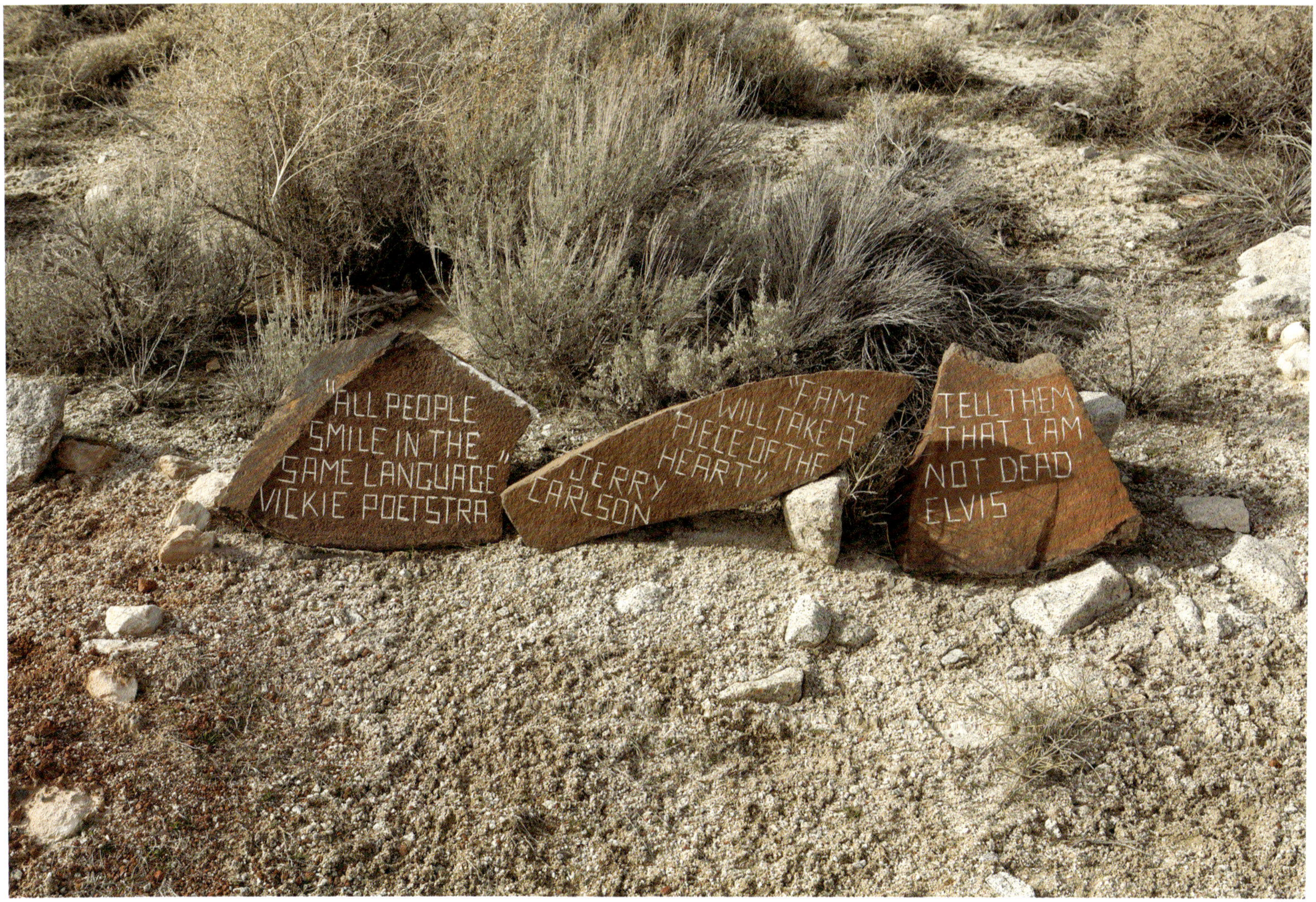
"ALL PEOPLE
SMILE IN THE
SAME LANGUAGE"
VICKIE POETSTRA
"FAME
WILL TAKE A
PIECE OF THE
HEART"
JERRY
CARLSON
TELL THEM
THAT I AM
NOT DEAD
ELVIS

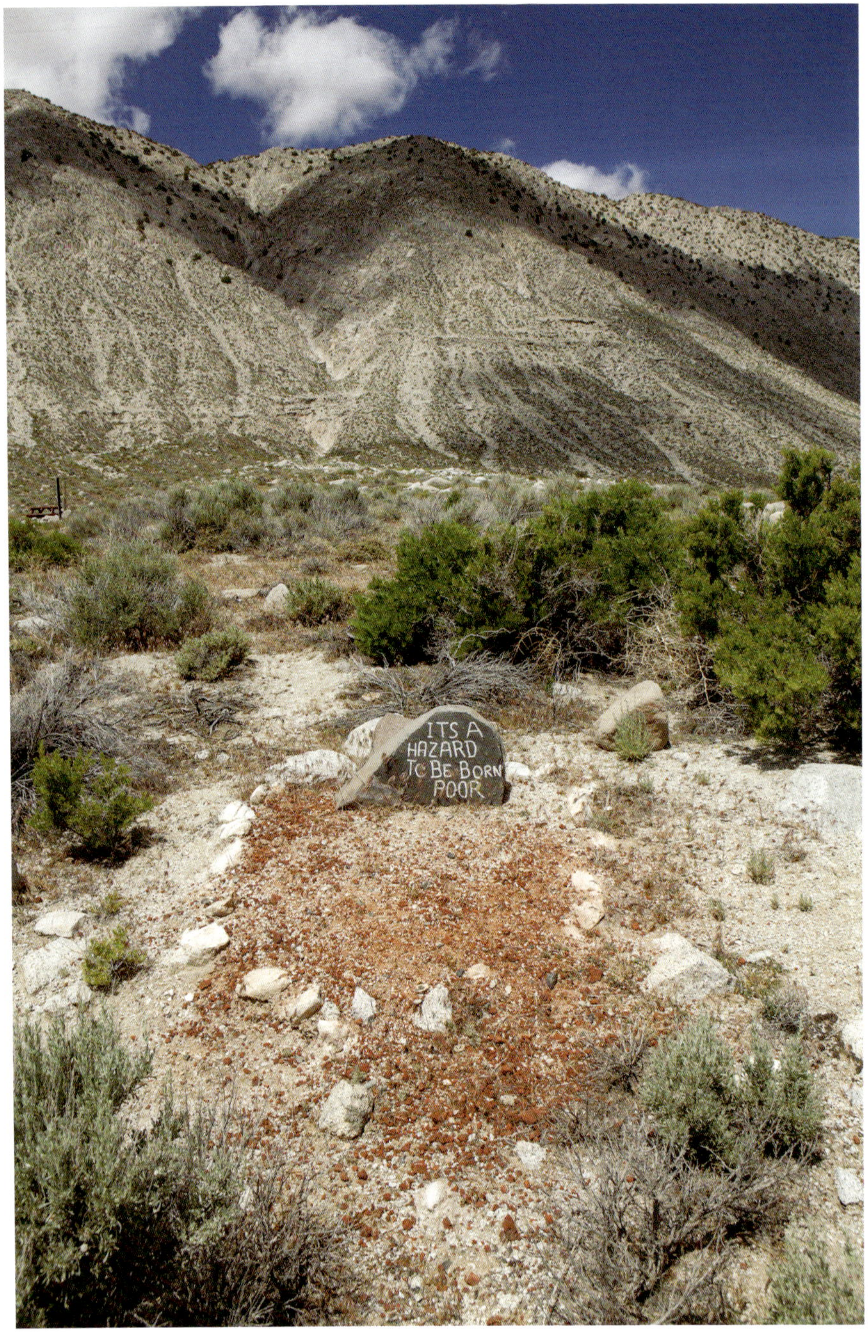
ITS A
HAZARD
TO BE BORN
POOR

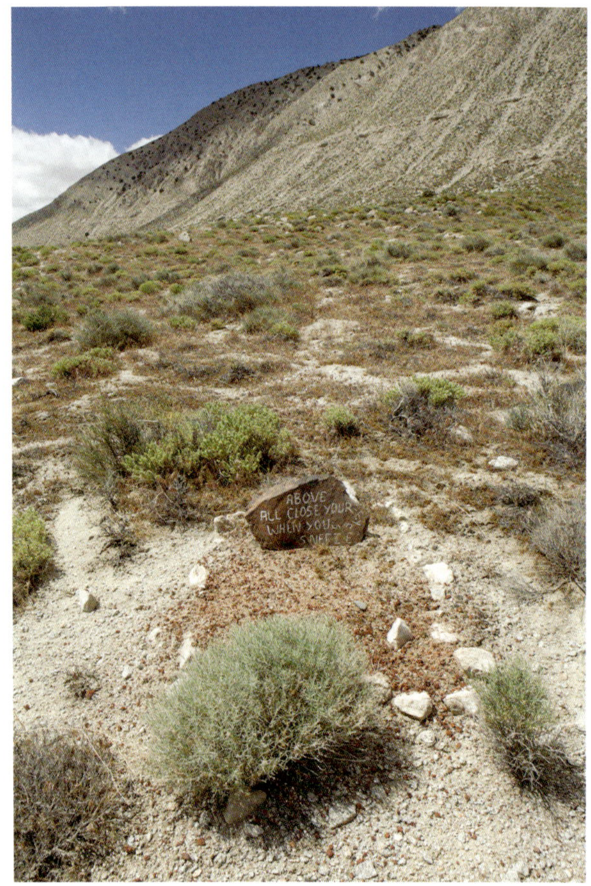
ABOVE
ALL CLOSE YOUR
WHEN YOU

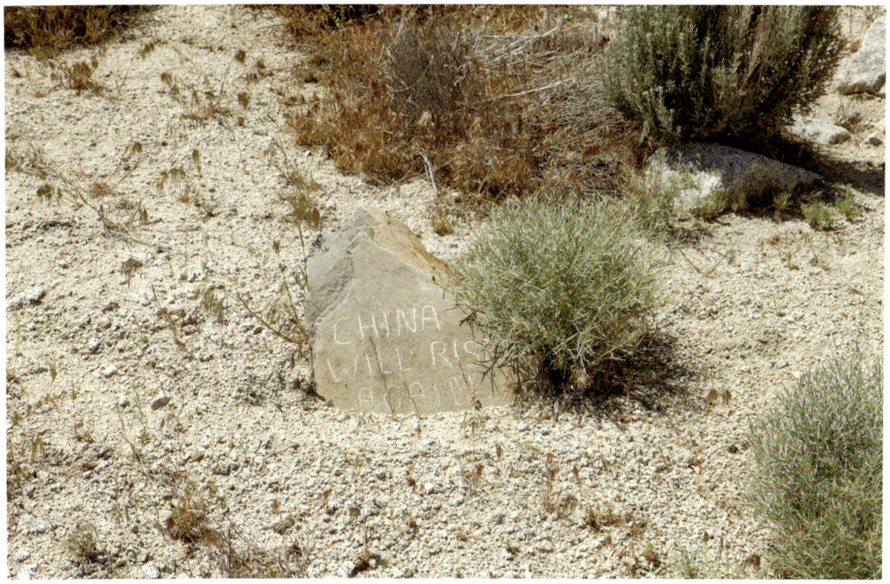
CHINA

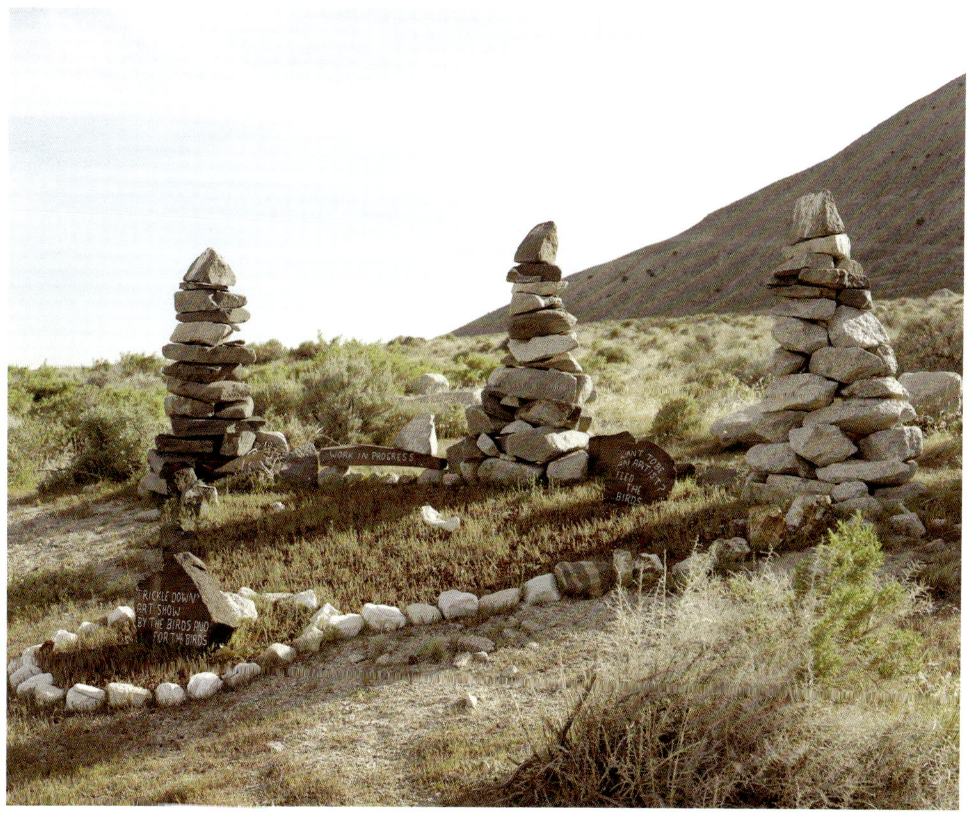
WORK IN PROGRESS
FEED THE BIRDS
TRICKLE DOWN ART SHOW BY THE BIRDS AND FOR THE BIRDS

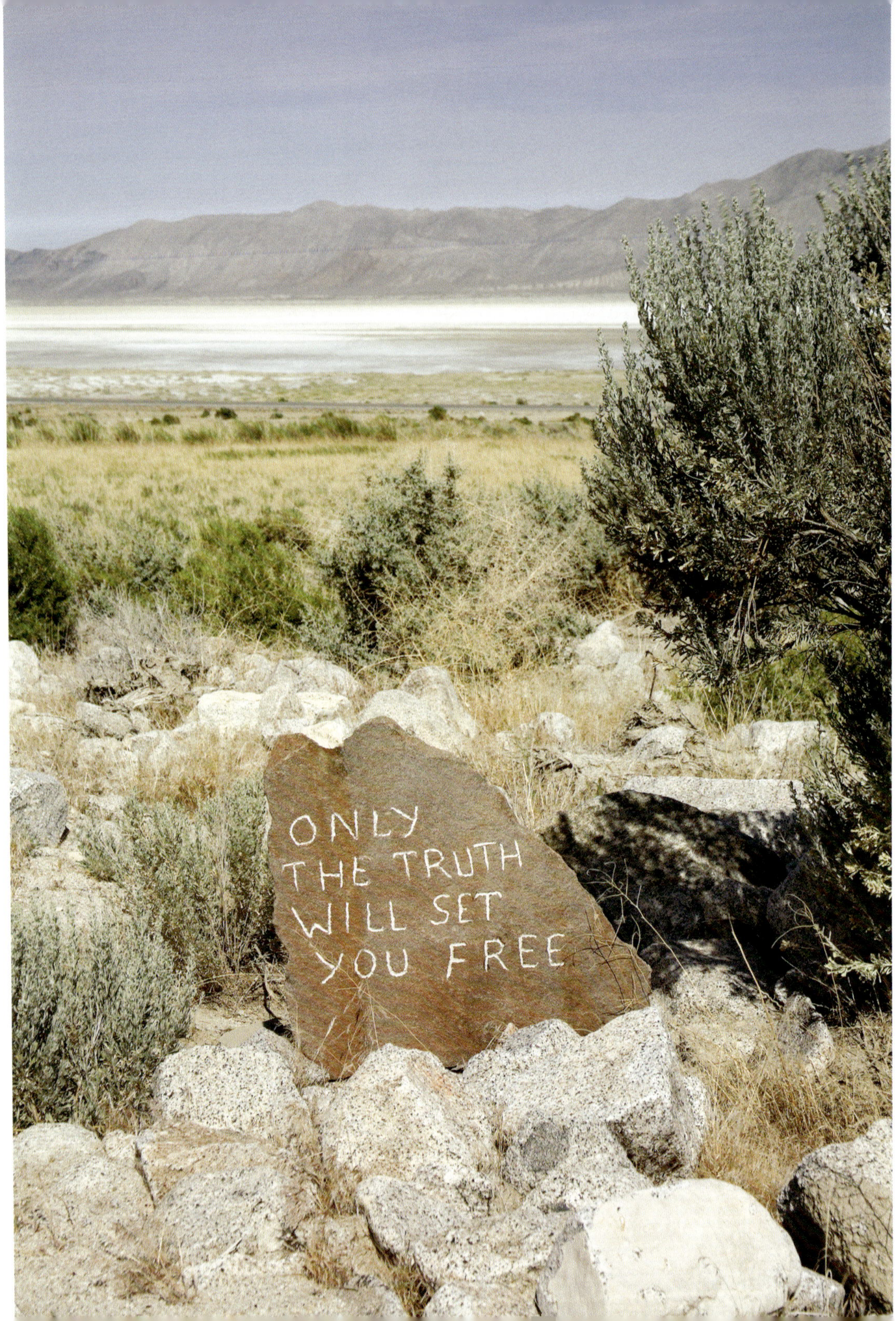
ONLY
THE TRUTH
WILL SET
YOU FREE

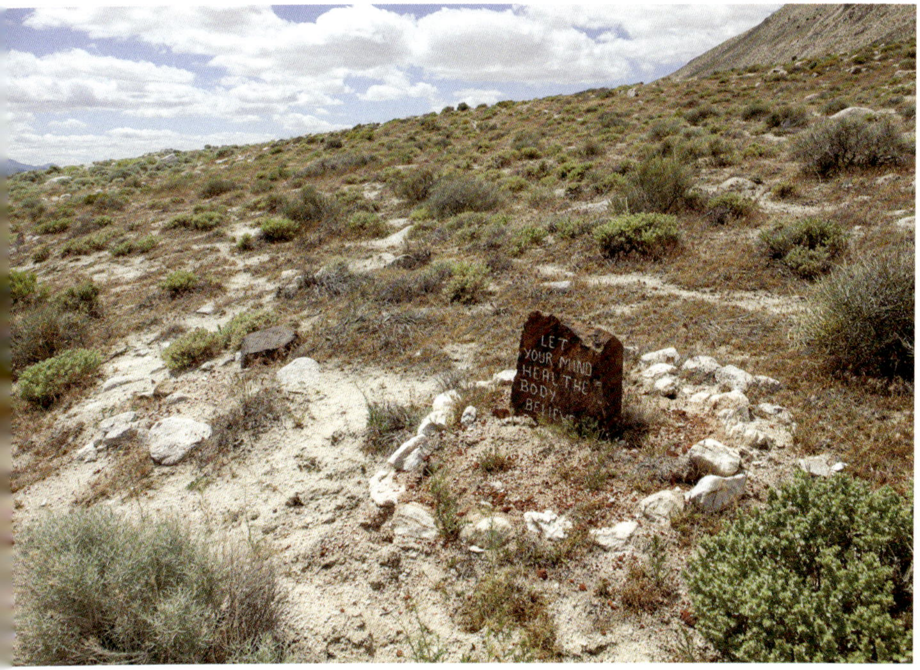
LET
YOUR MIND
HEAL THE
BODY

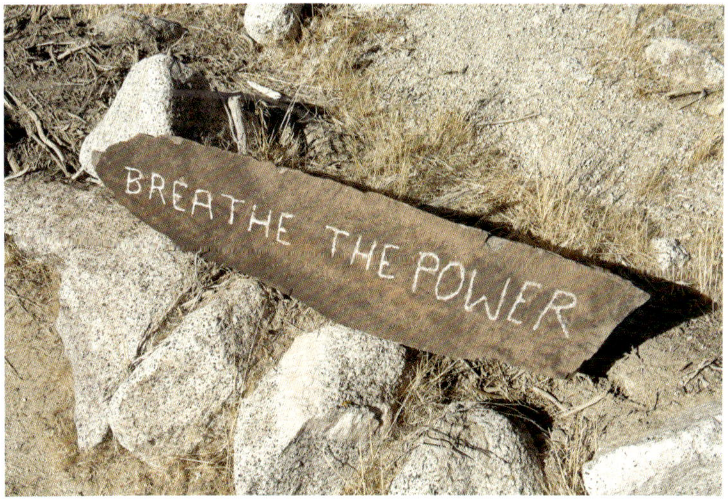
BREATHE THE POWER

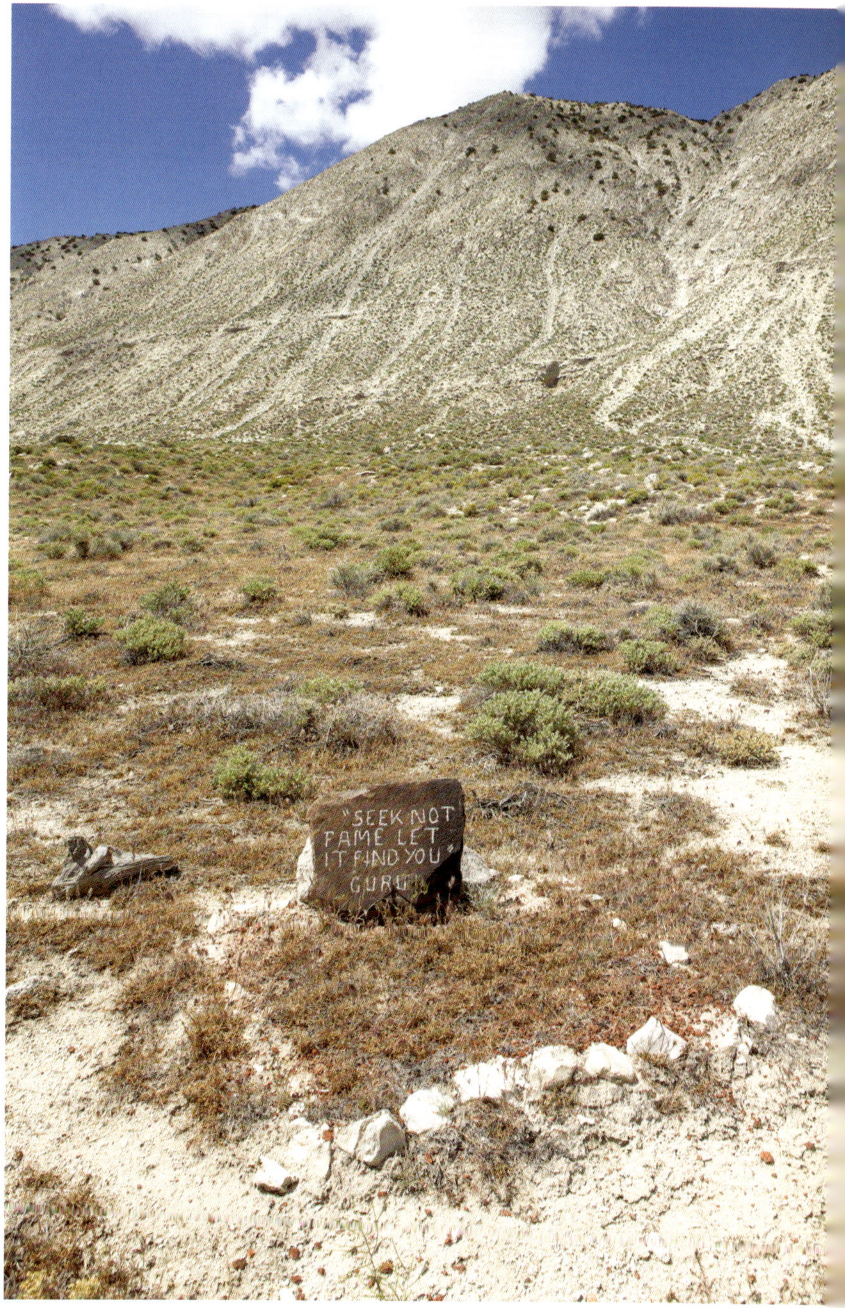
"SEEK NOT
FAME LET
IT FIND YOU"
GURU

30 |

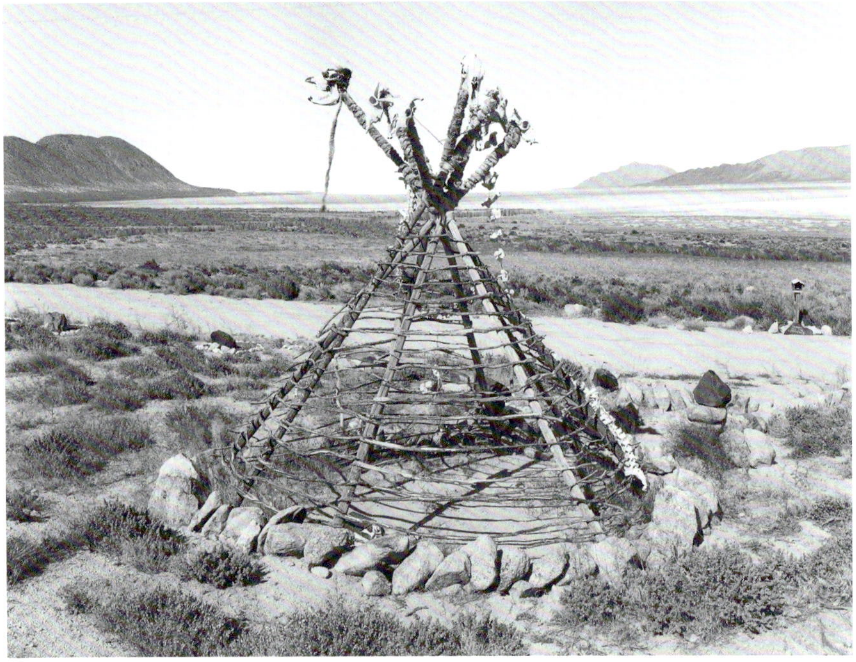

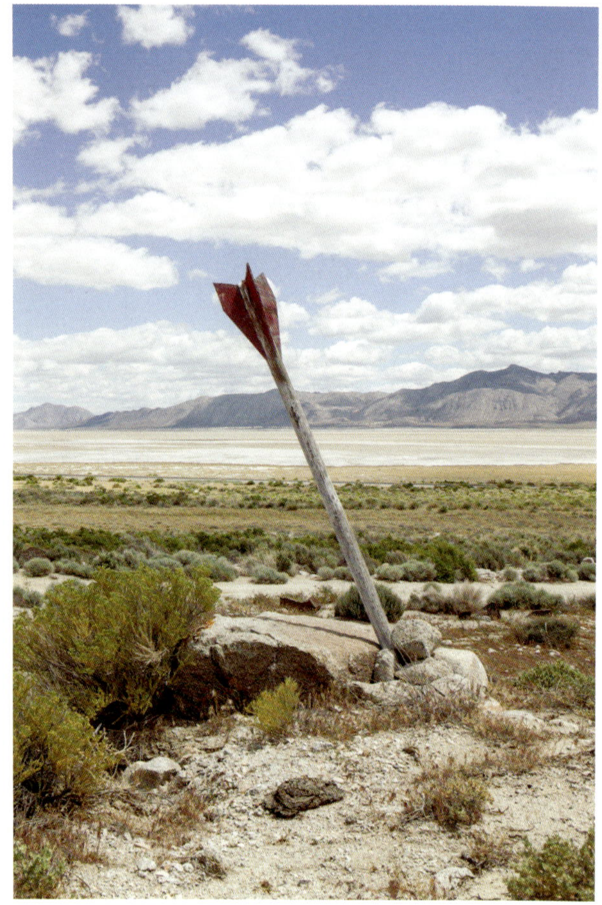

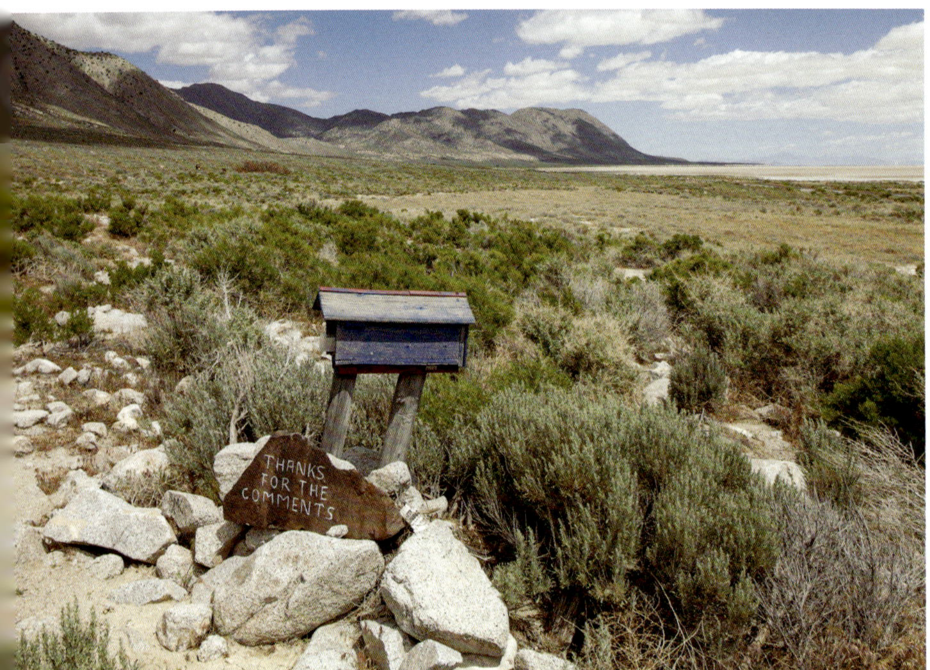

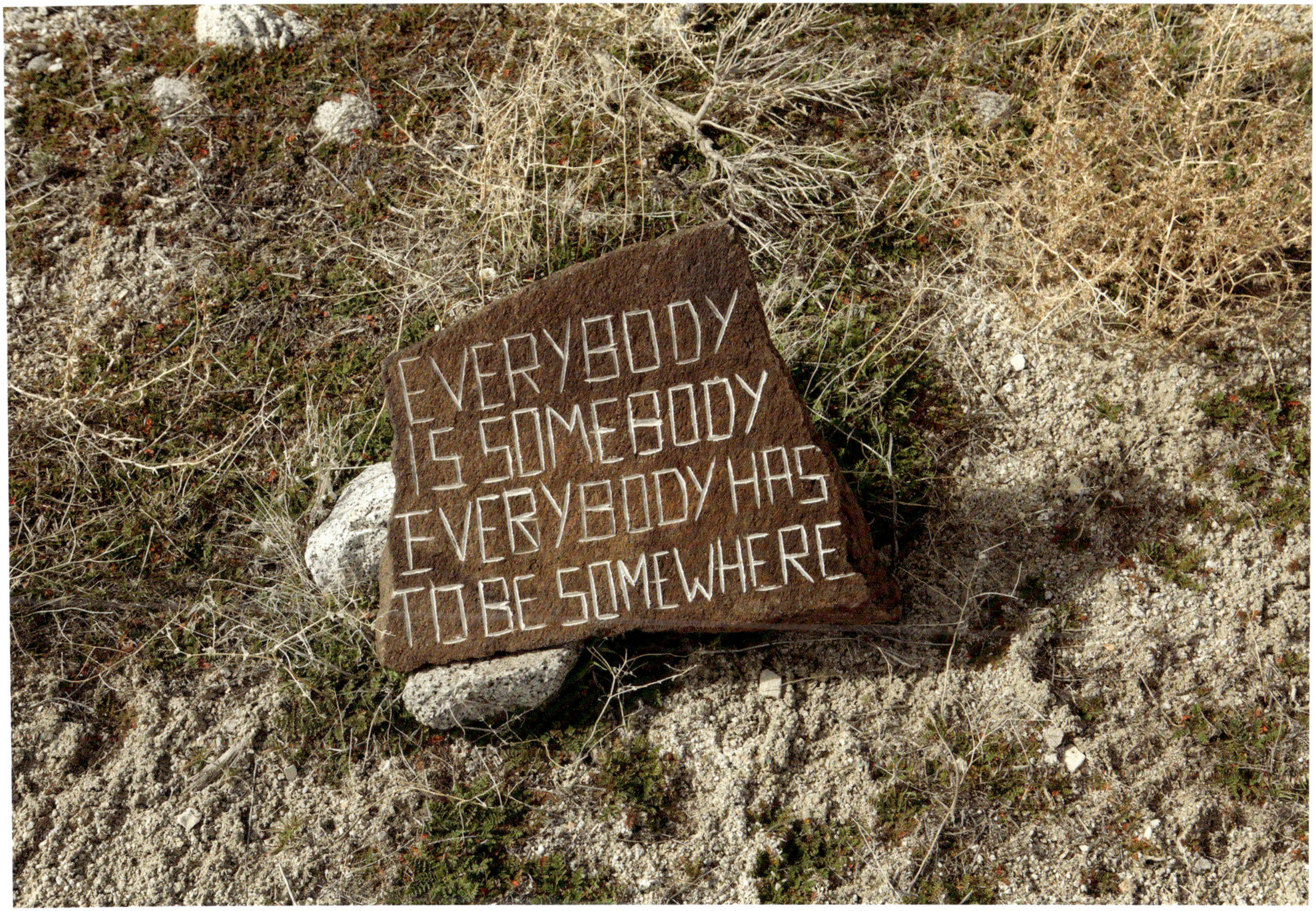
EVERYBODY
IS SOMEBODY
EVERYBODY HAS
TO BE SOMEWHERE

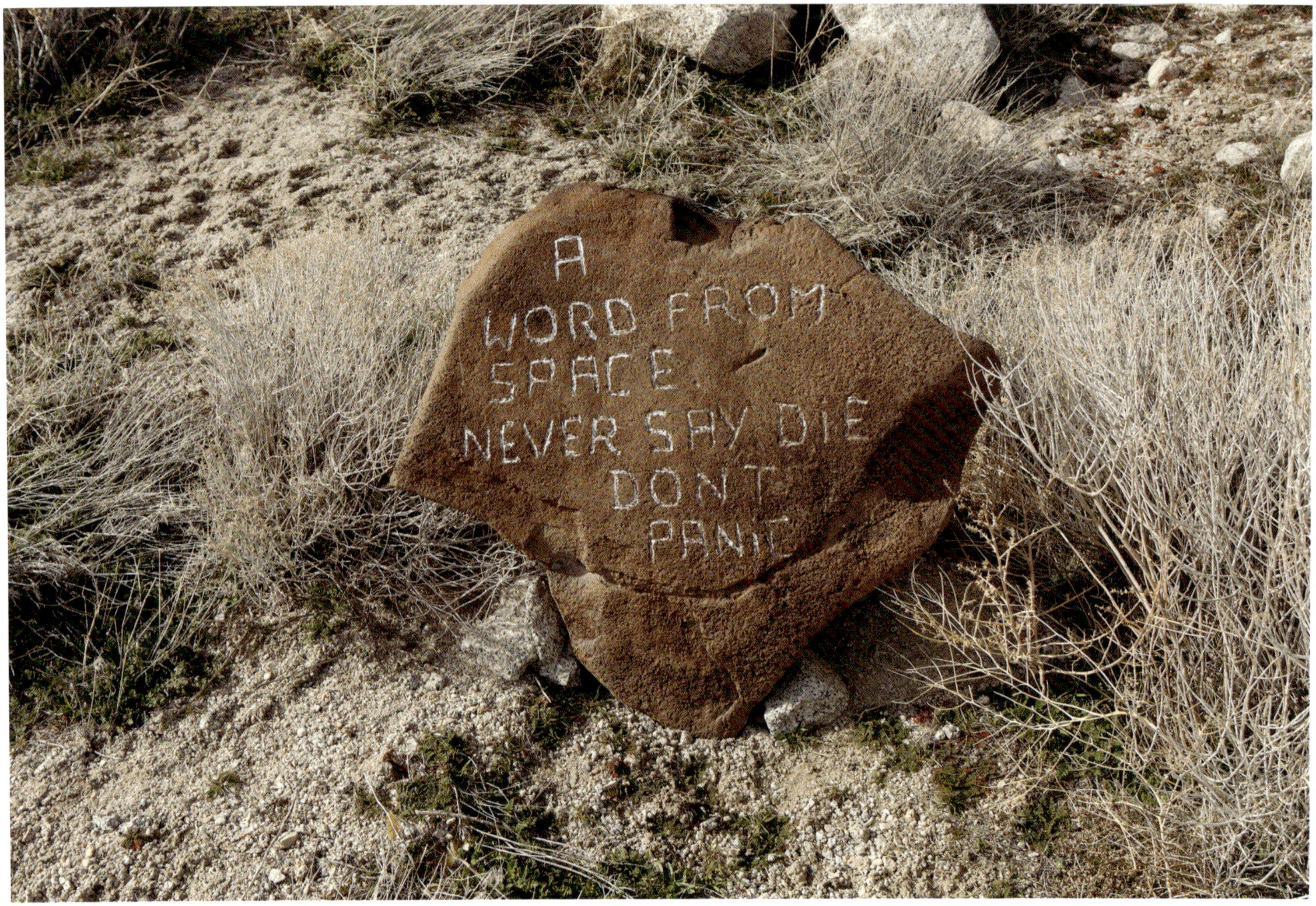
A
WORD FROM
SPACE
NEVER SAY DIE
DONT
PANIC

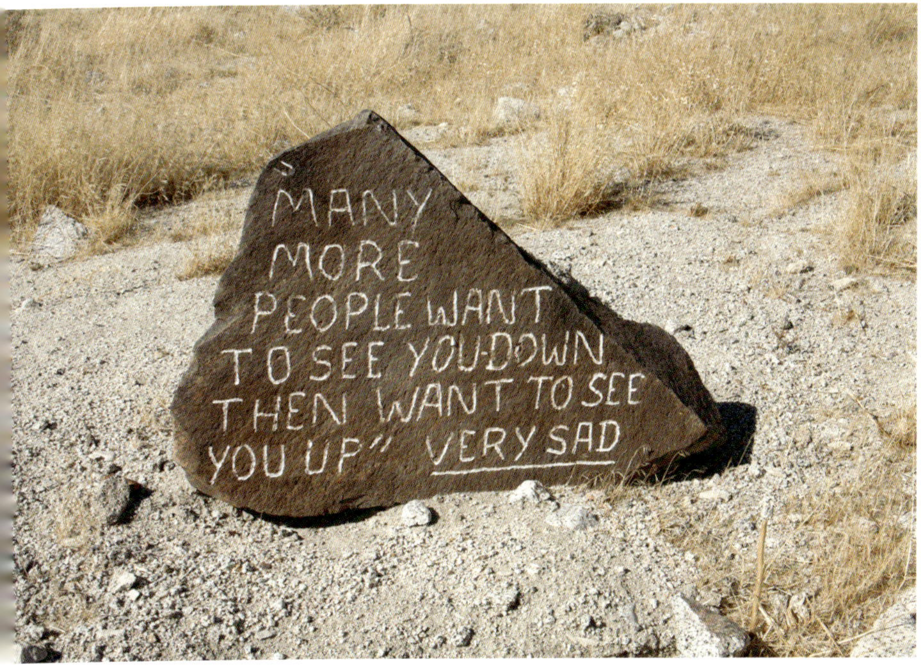
"MANY
MORE
PEOPLE WANT
TO SEE YOU DOWN
THEN WANT TO SEE
YOU UP" VERY SAD

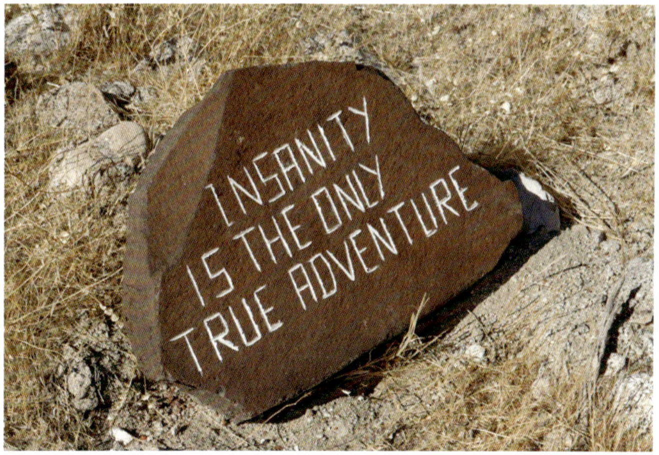
INSANITY
IS THE ONLY
TRUE ADVENTURE

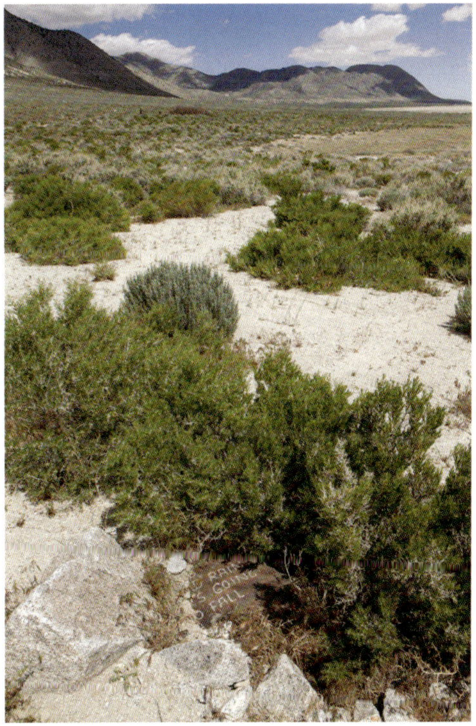

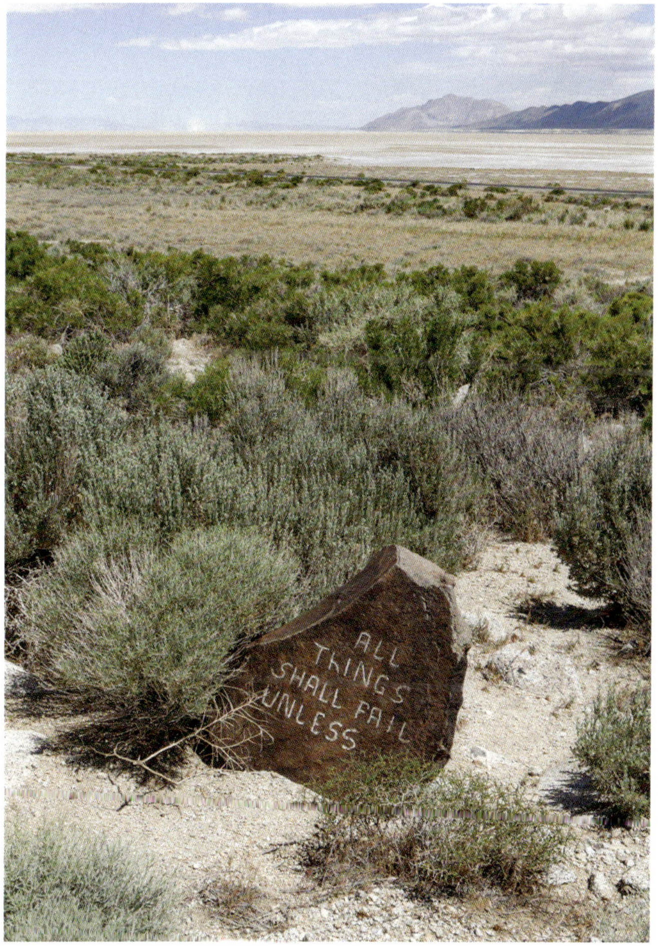
ALL
THINGS
SHALL FAIL
UNLESS

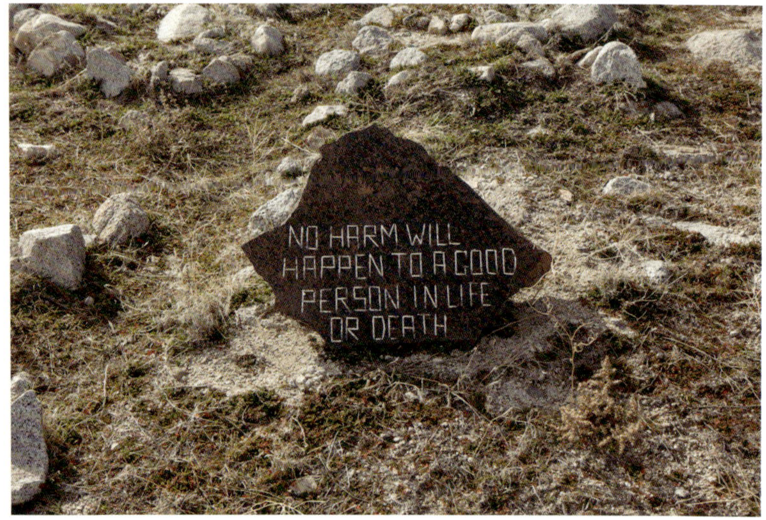
NO HARM WILL
HAPPEN TO A GOOD
PERSON IN LIFE
OR DEATH

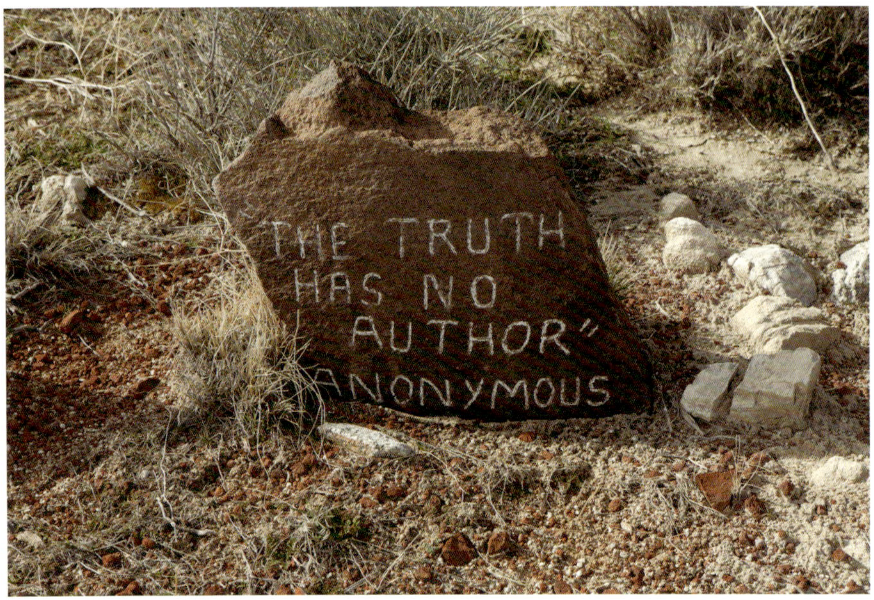
"THE TRUTH
HAS NO
AUTHOR"
ANONYMOUS

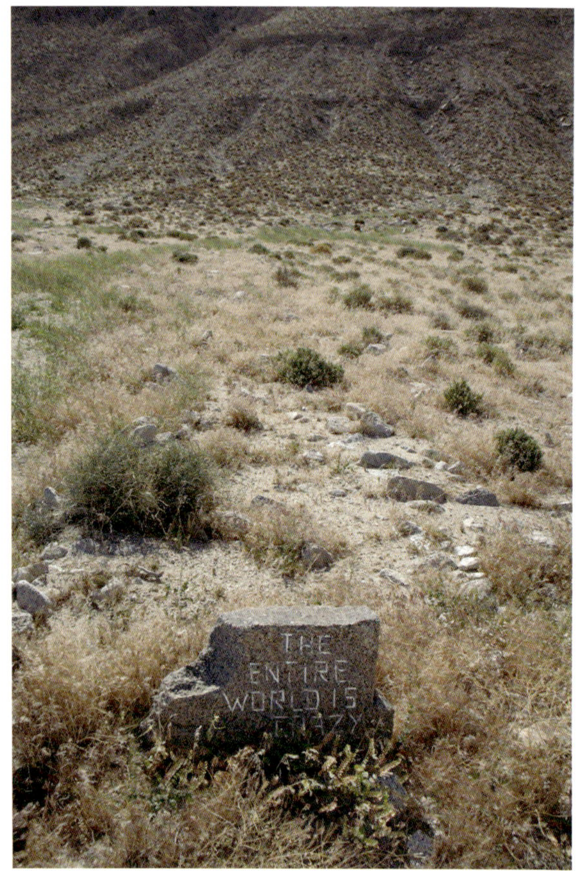
THE
ENTIRE
WORLD IS

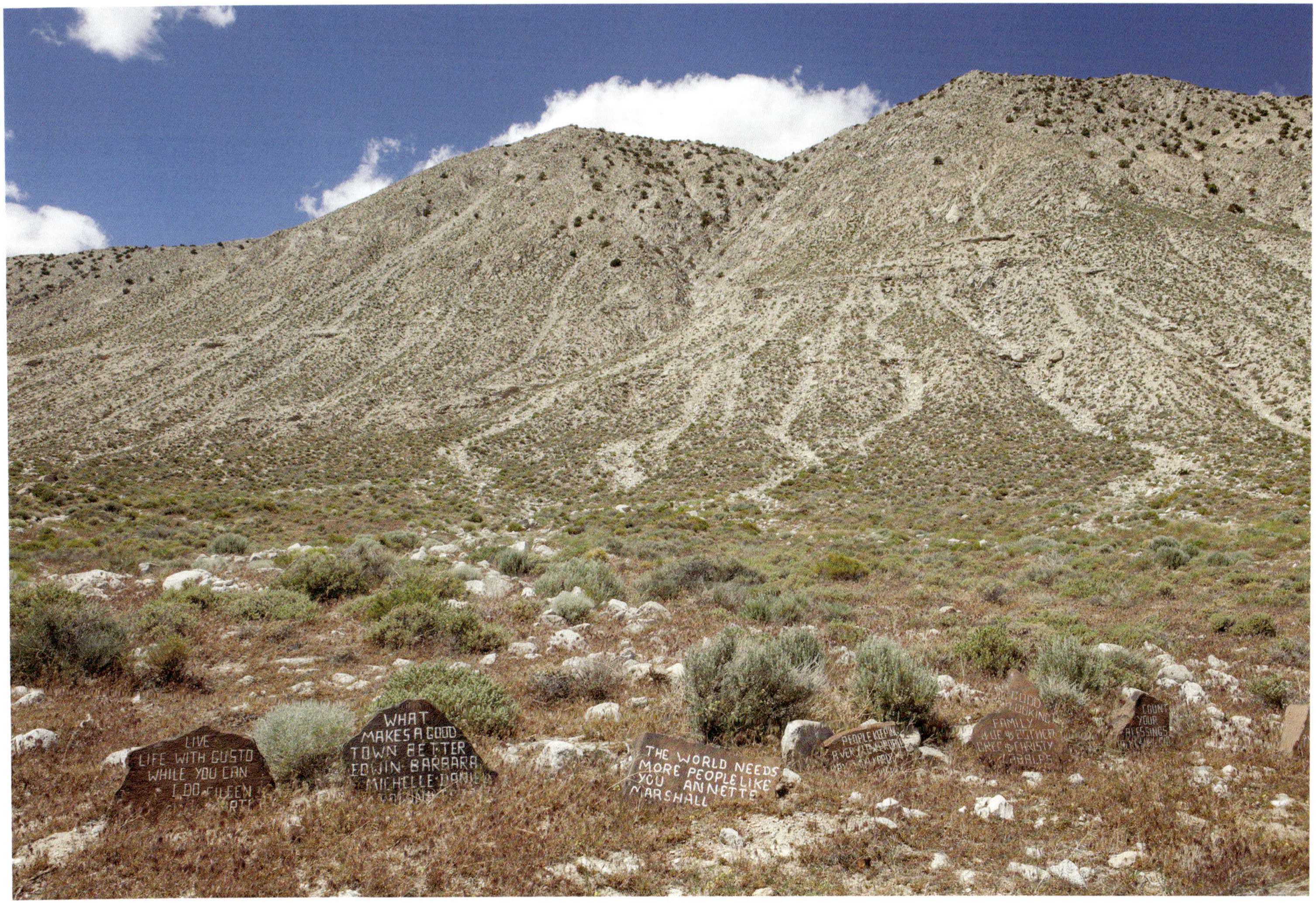
LIVE
LIFE WITH GUSTO
WHILE YOU CAN
WHAT
MAKES A GOOD
TOWN BETTER
EDWIN BARBARA
THE WORLD NEEDS
MORE PEOPLE LIKE
YOU ANNETTE
MARSHALL

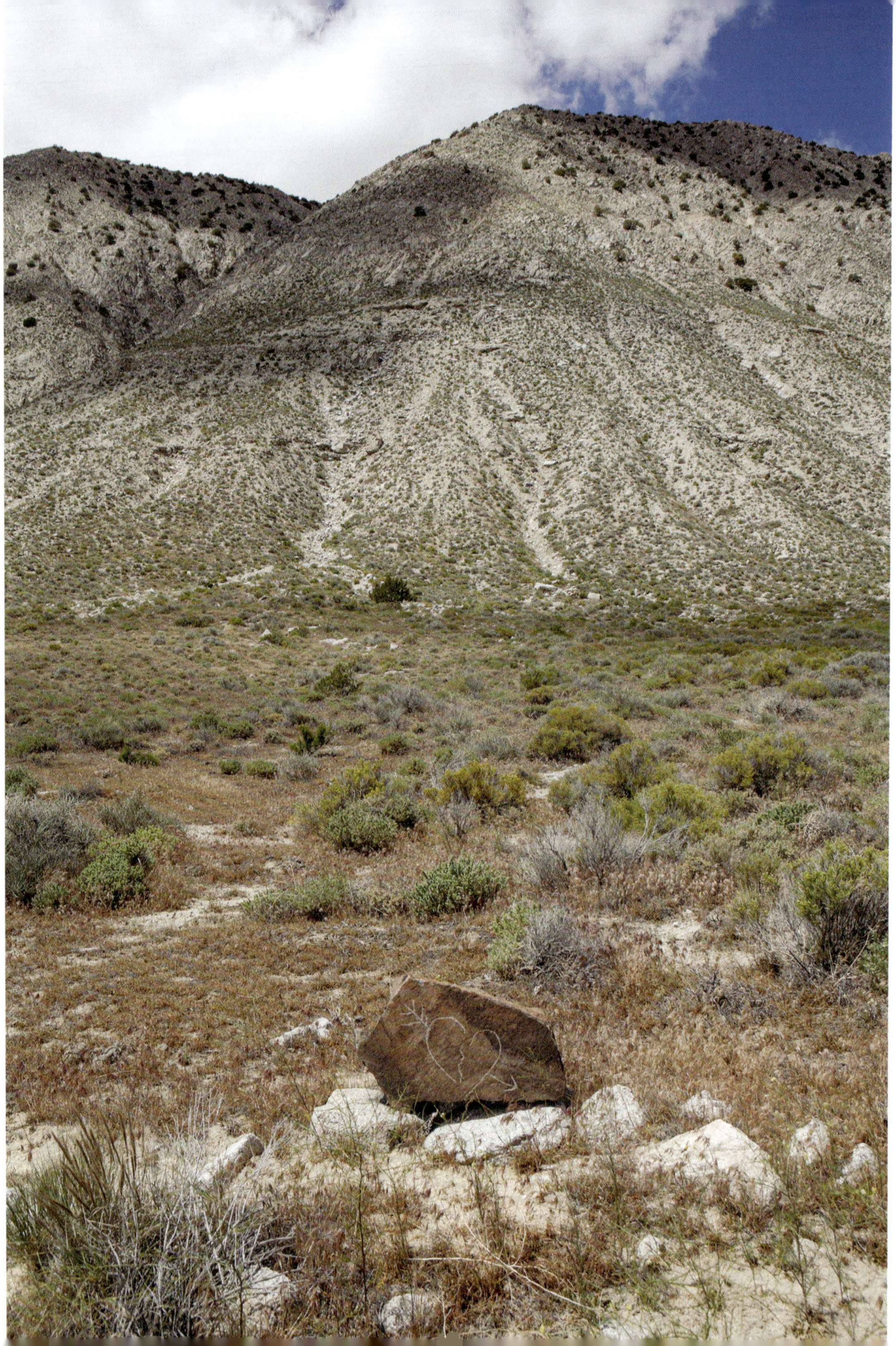

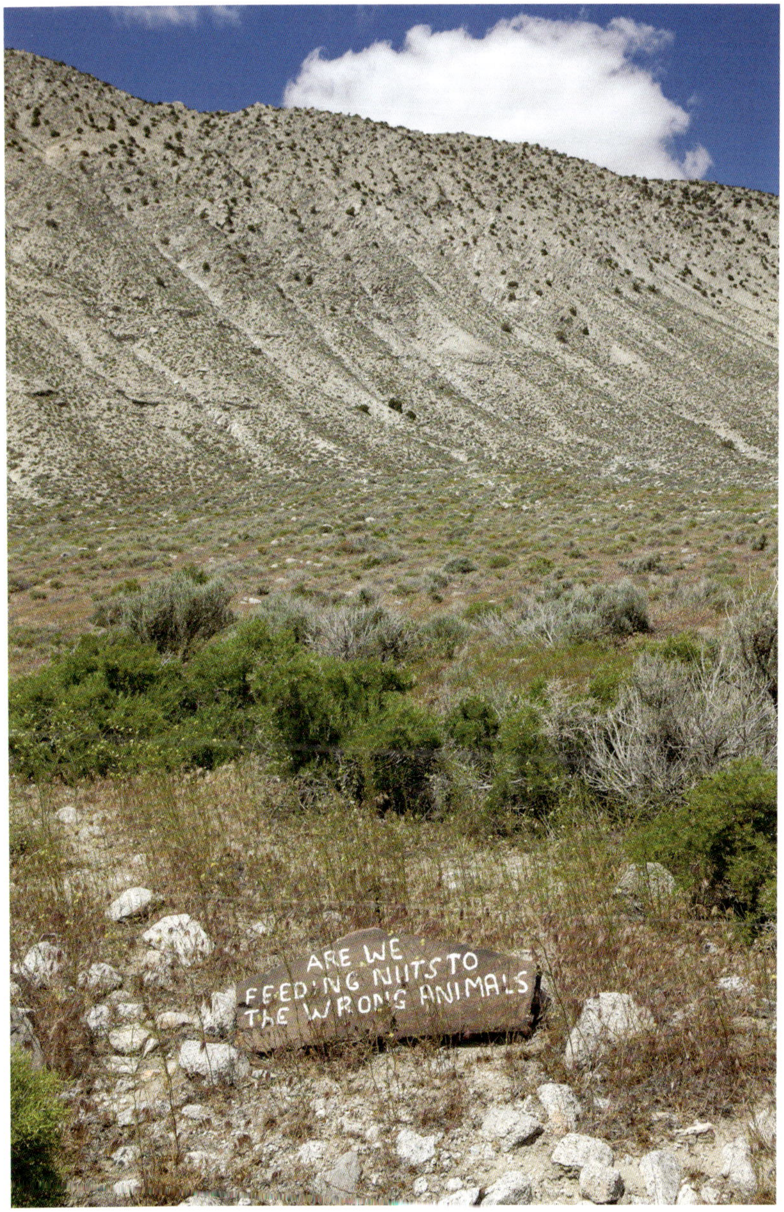
ARE WE
FEEDING NUTS TO
THE WRONG ANIMALS

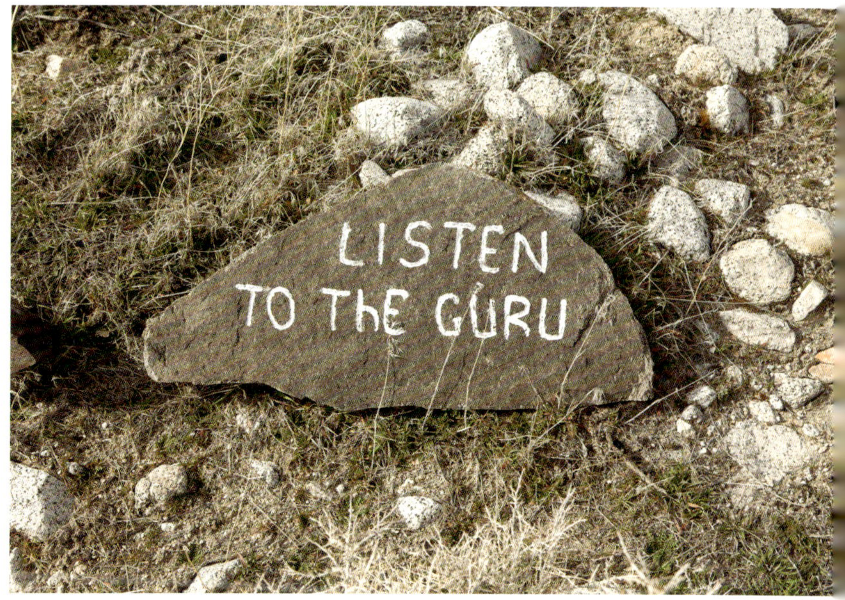
LISTEN
TO THE GURU

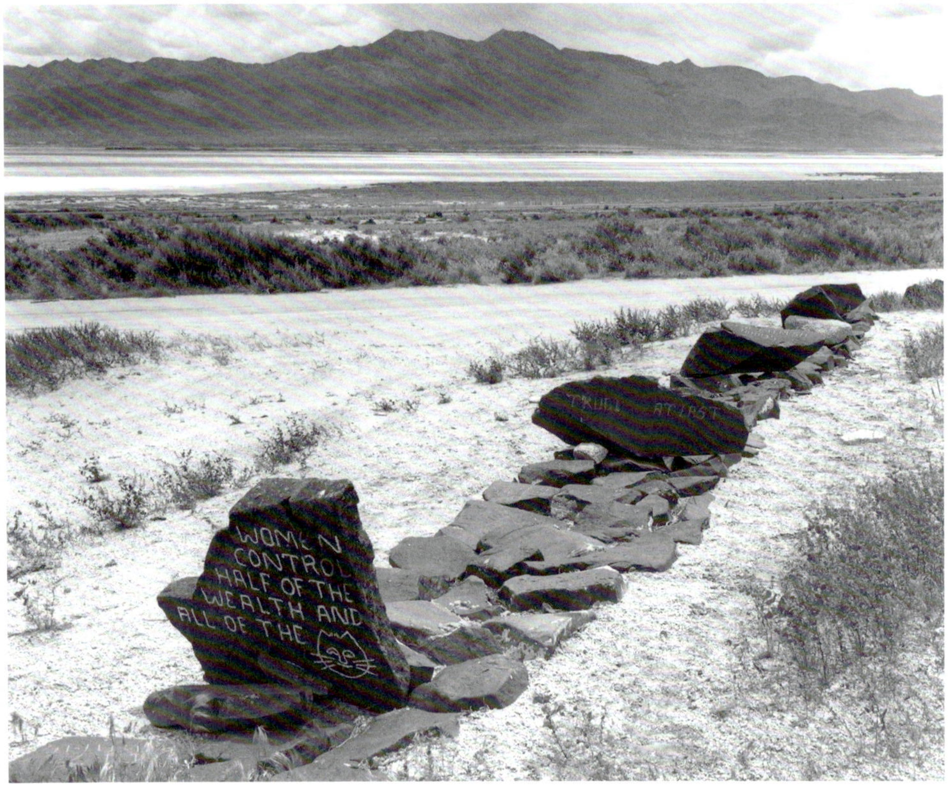
WOMEN
CONTROL
HALF OF THE
WEALTH AND
ALL OF THE

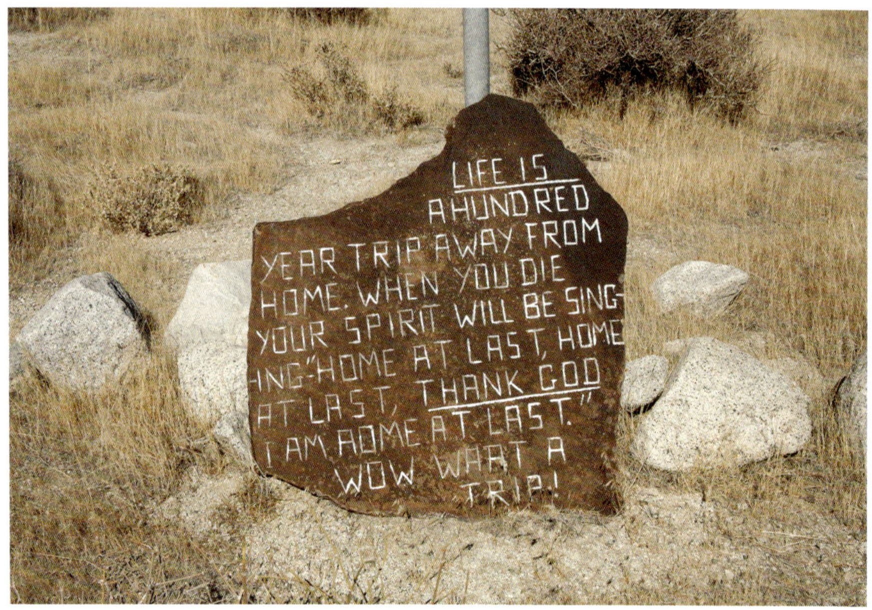
LIFE IS
A HUNDRED
YEAR TRIP AWAY FROM
HOME. WHEN YOU DIE
YOUR SPIRIT WILL BE SING-
ING "HOME AT LAST, HOME
AT LAST, THANK GOD
I AM HOME AT LAST."
WOW WHAT A
TRIP!

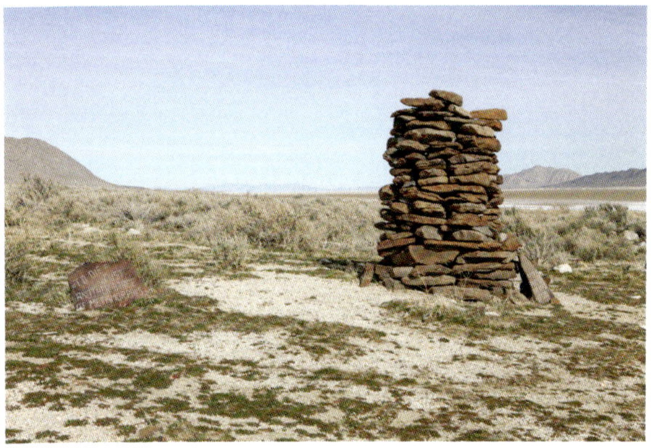

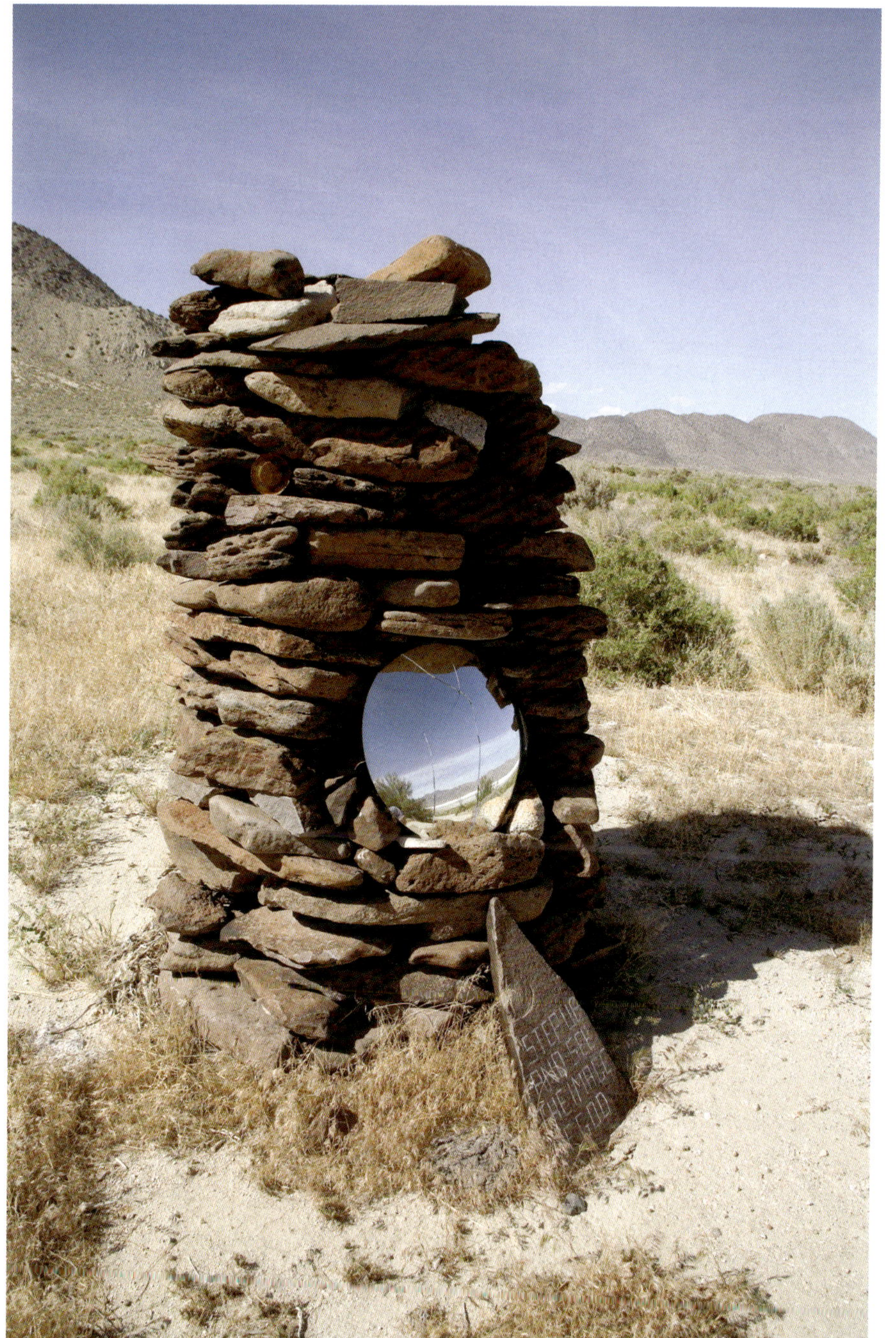

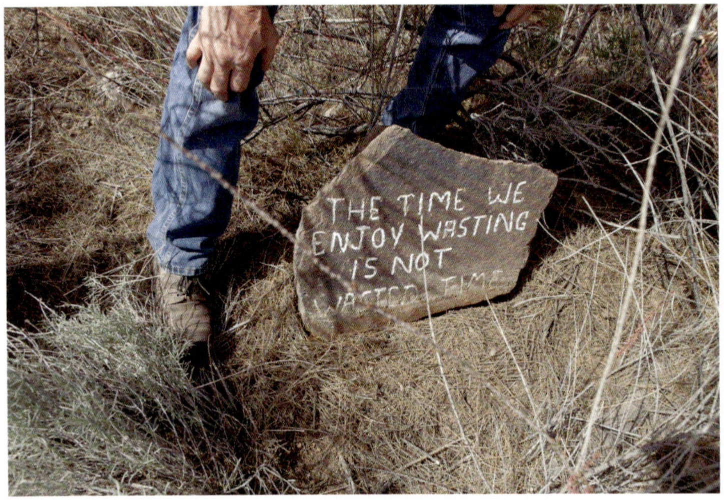
THE TIME WE
ENJOY WASTING
IS NOT

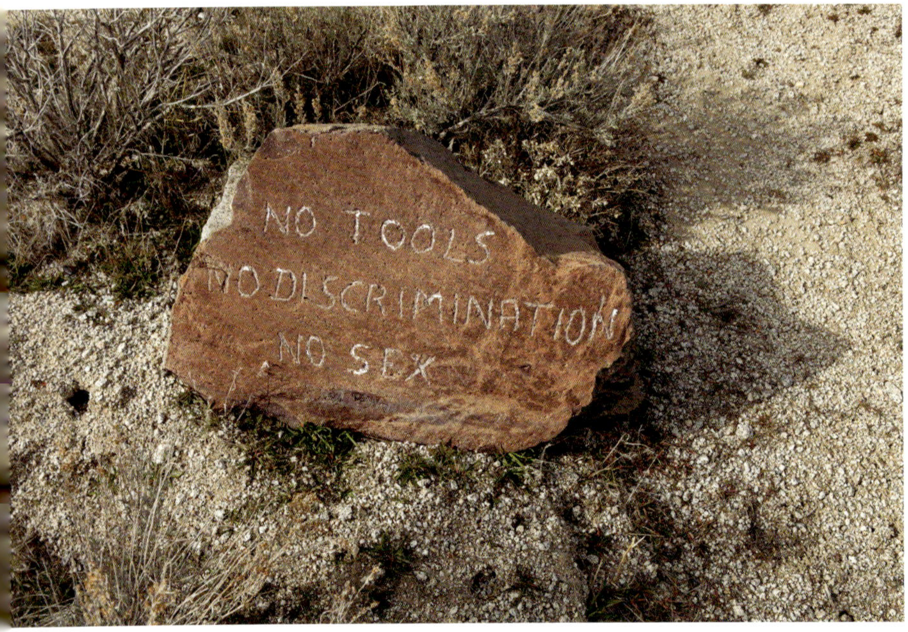
NO TOOLS
NO DISCRIMINATION
NO SEX

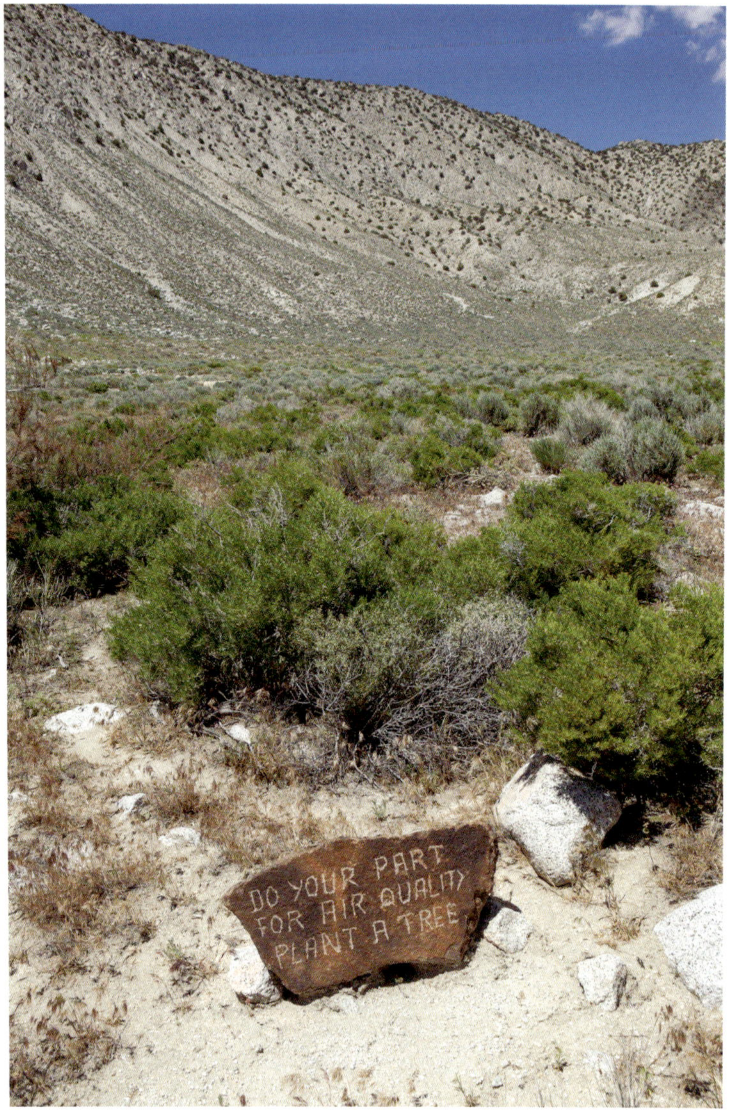
DO YOUR PART
FOR AIR QUALITY
PLANT A TREE

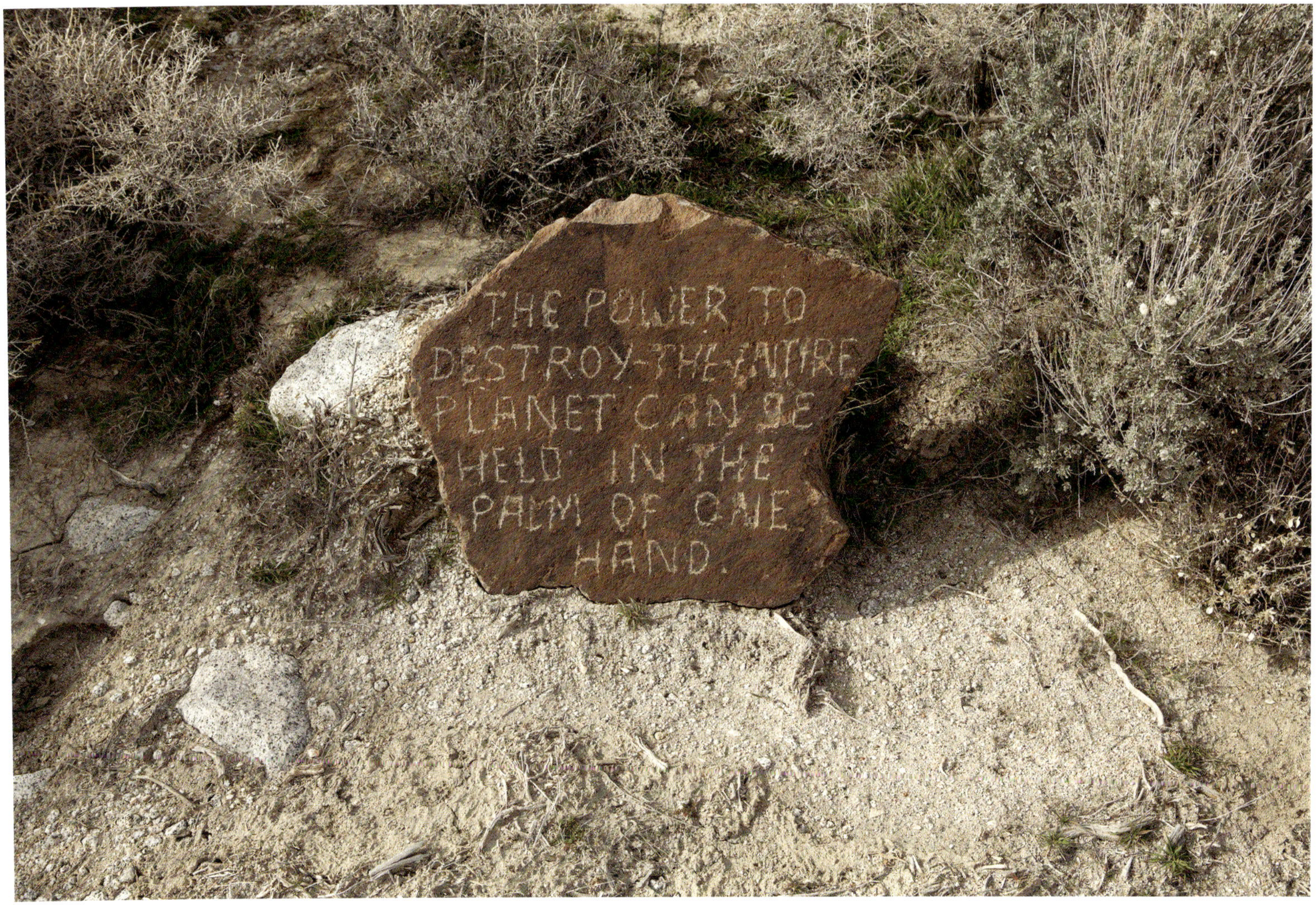
THE POWER TO
DESTROY THE ENTIRE
PLANET CAN BE
HELD IN THE
PALM OF ONE
HAND.

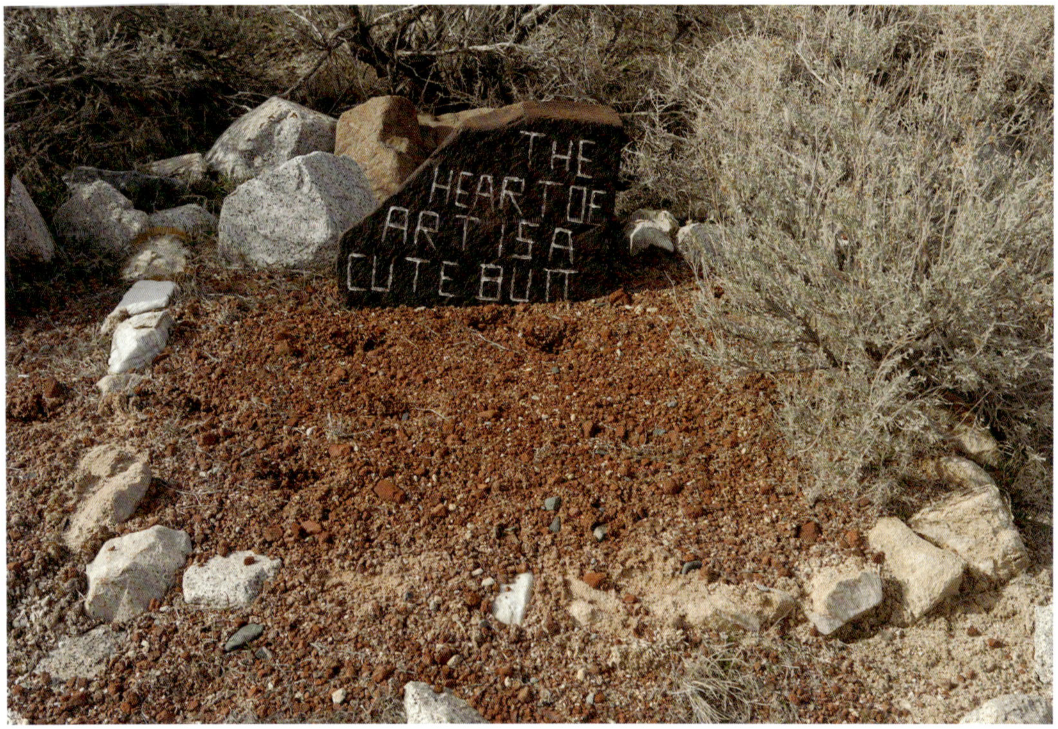
THE
HEART OF
ART IS A
CUTE BUTT

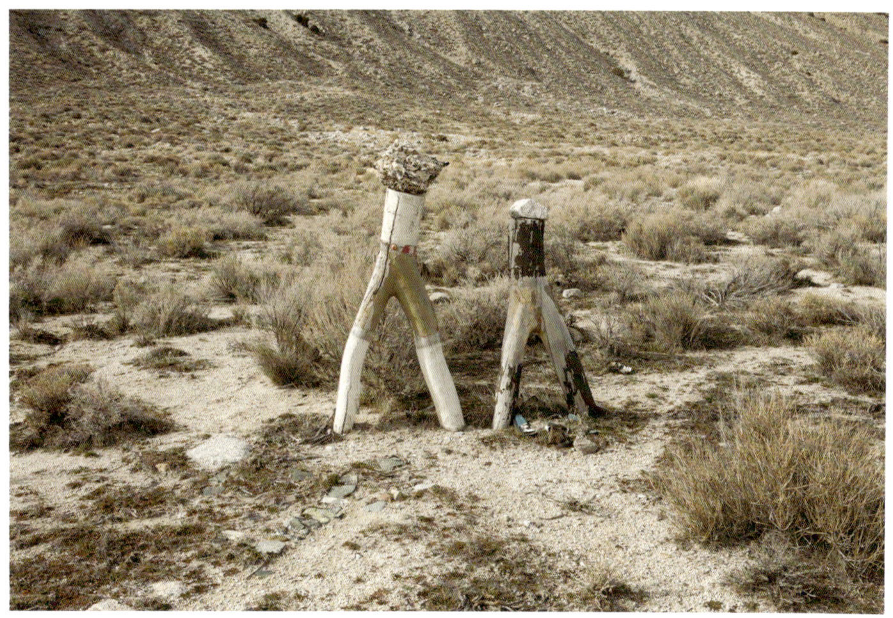

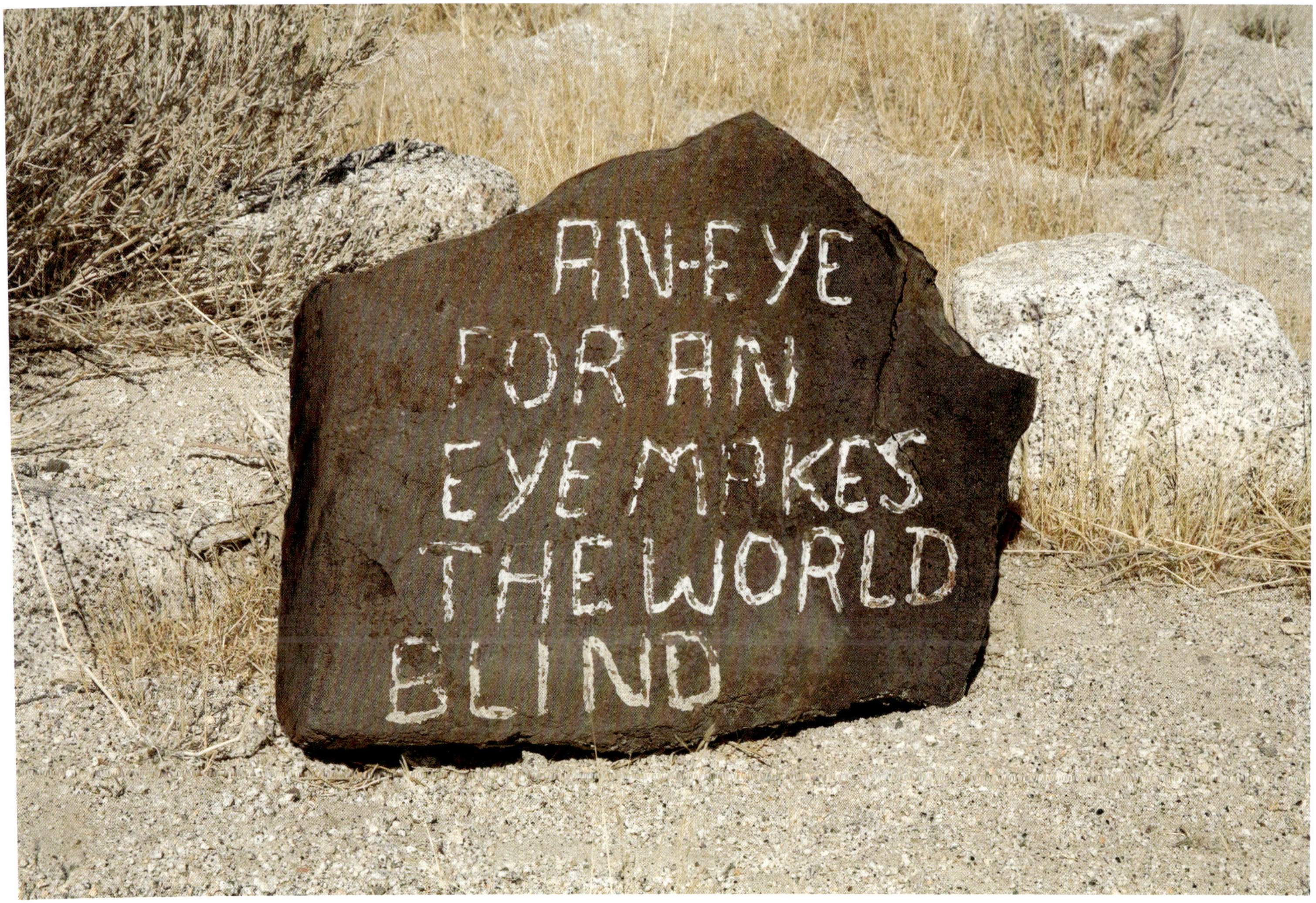
AN-EYE
FOR AN
EYE MAKES
THE WORLD
BLIND

50

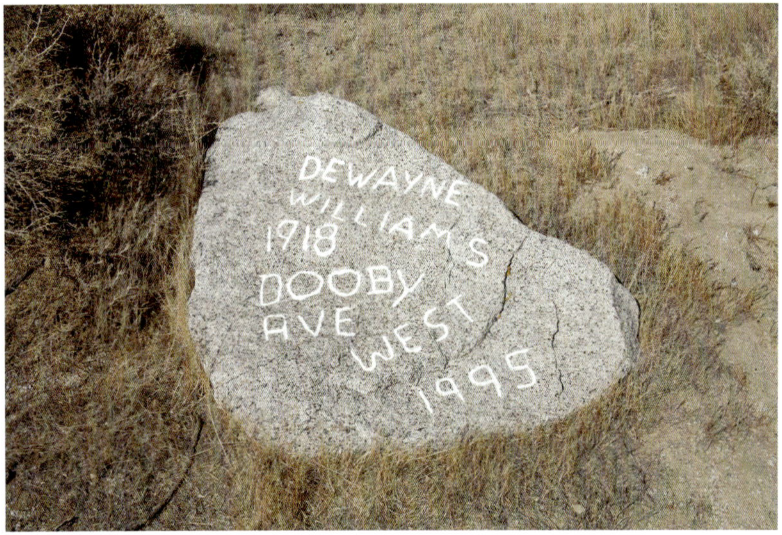
DEWAYNE
WILLIAMS
1918
DOOBY
AVE
WEST
1995

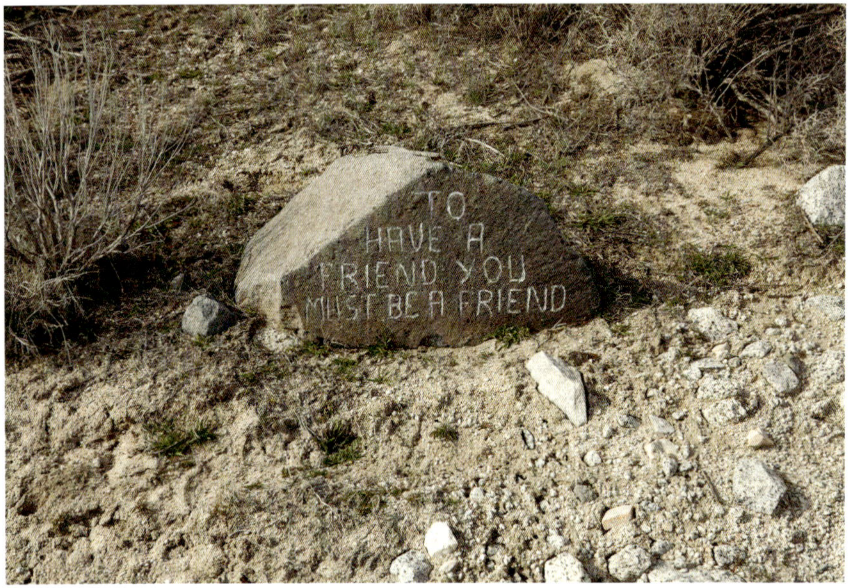
TO
HAVE A
FRIEND YOU
MUST BE A FRIEND

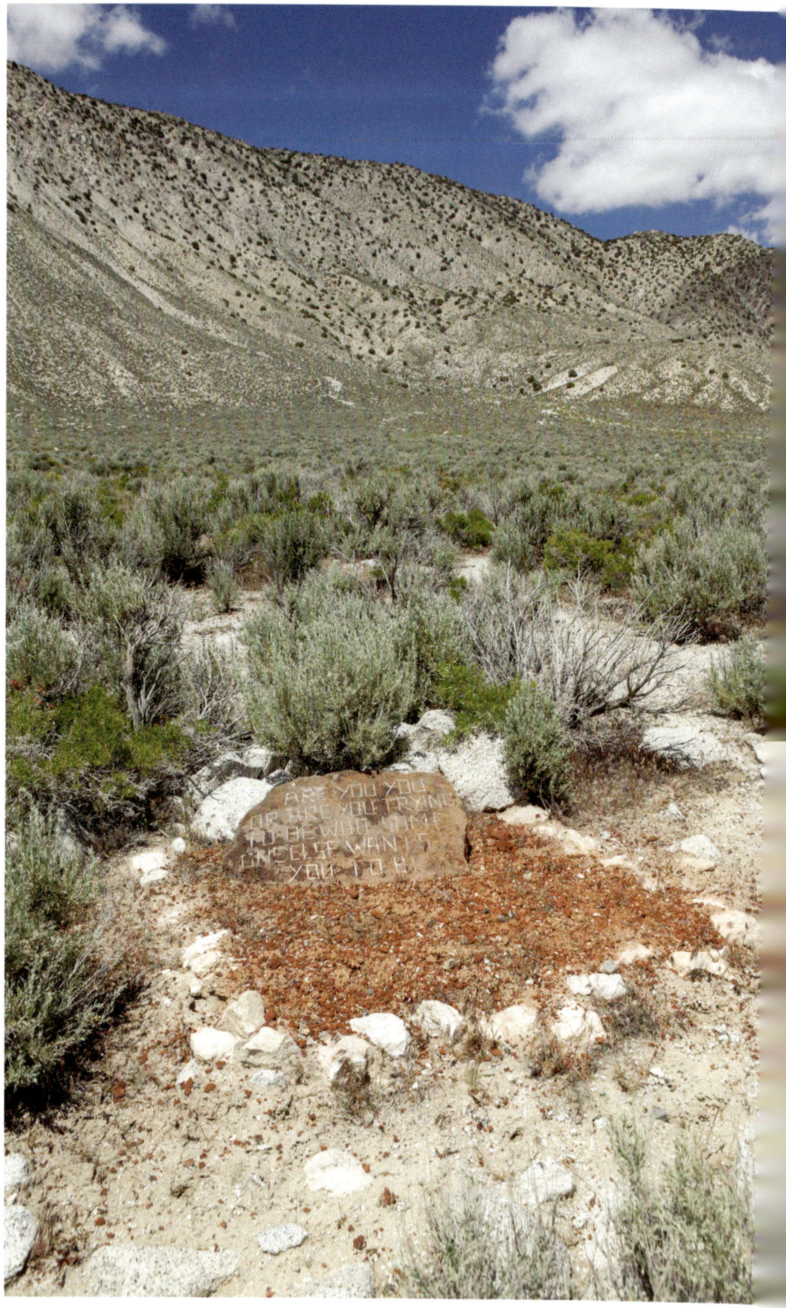
ARE YOU YOU
OR ARE YOU TRYING

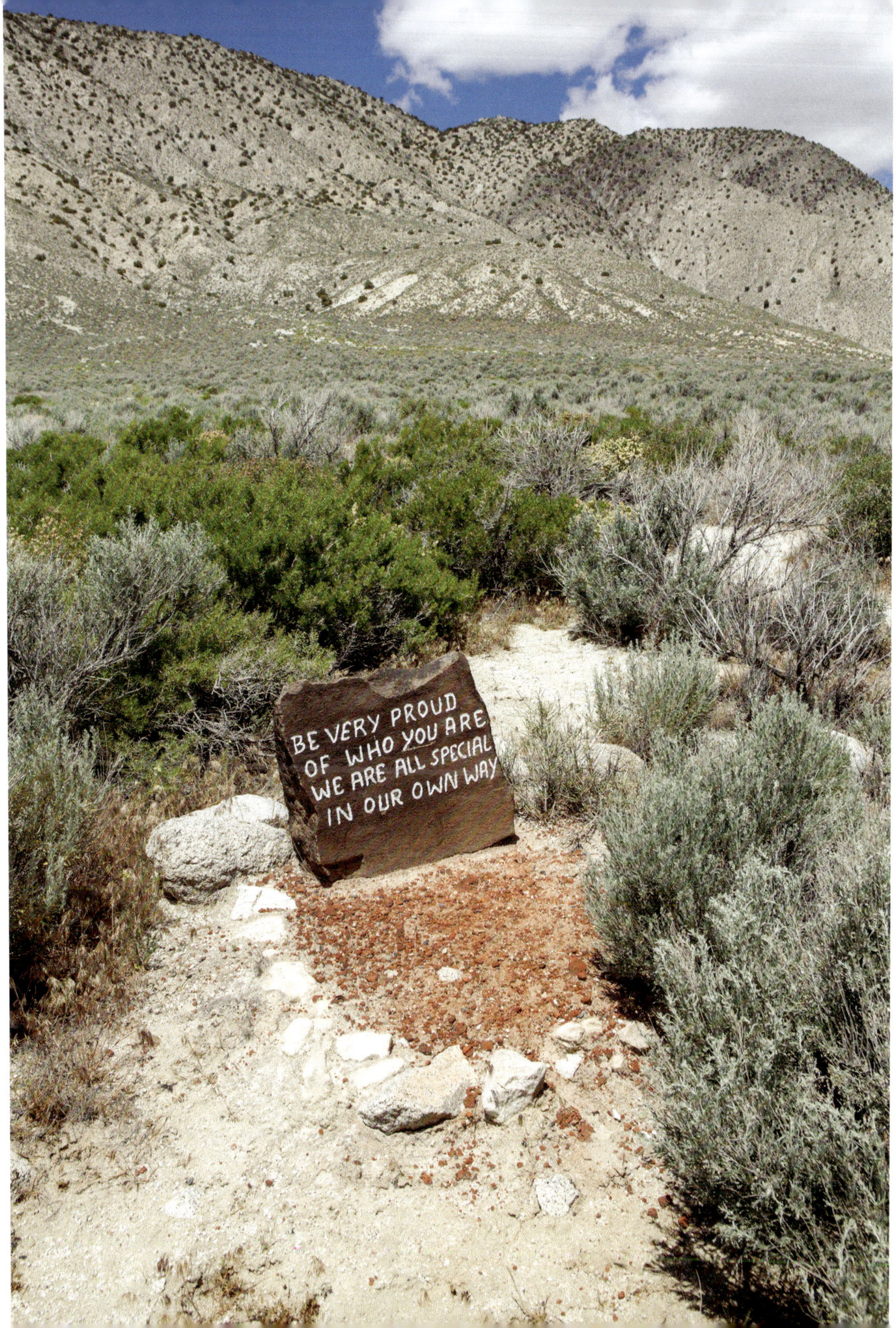
BE VERY PROUD
OF WHO YOU ARE
WE ARE ALL SPECIAL
IN OUR OWN WAY

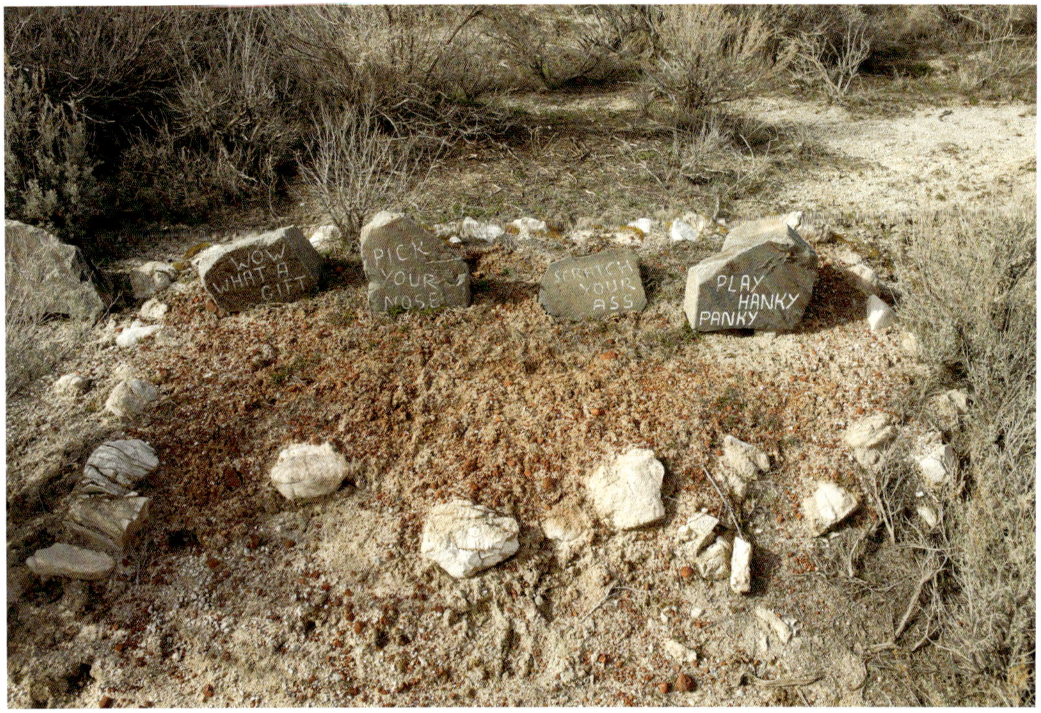
WOW WHAT A GIFT
PICK YOUR NOSE
SCRATCH YOUR ASS
PLAY HANKY PANKY

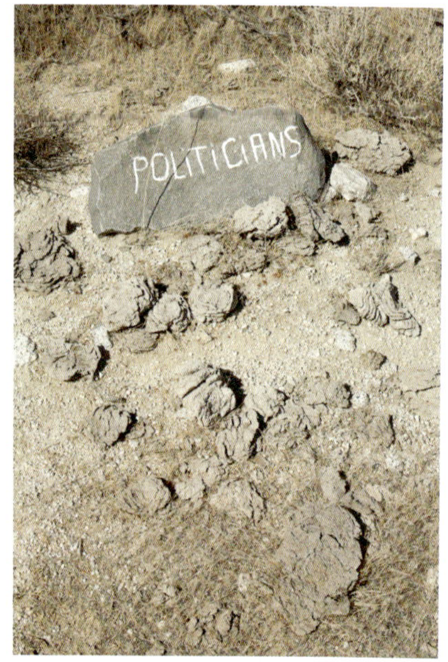
POLITICIANS

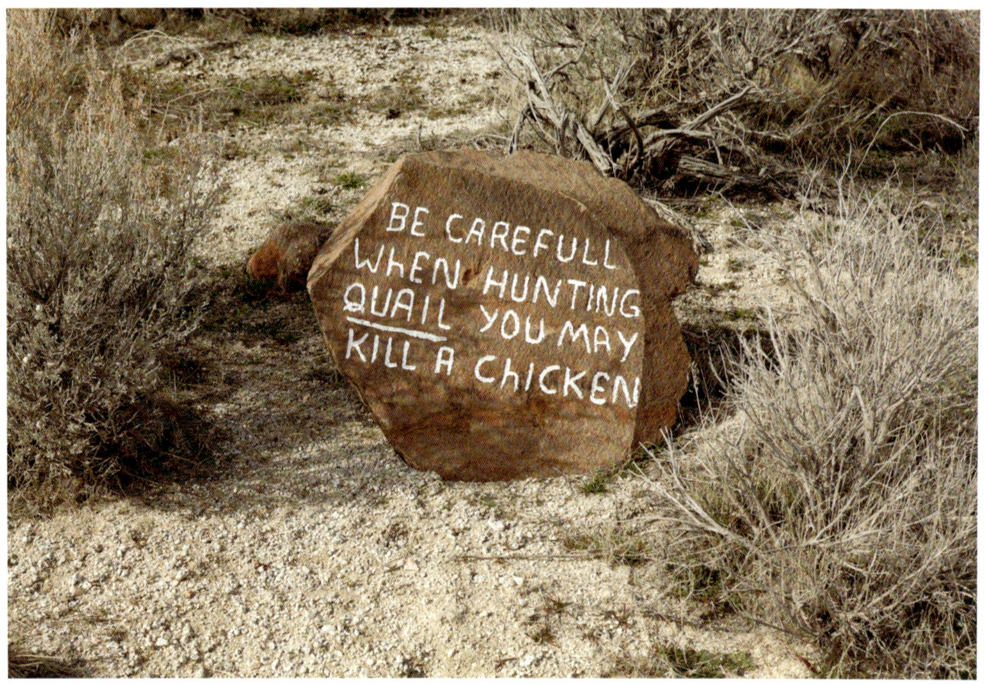
BE CAREFULL
WHEN HUNTING
QUAIL YOU MAY
KILL A CHICKEN

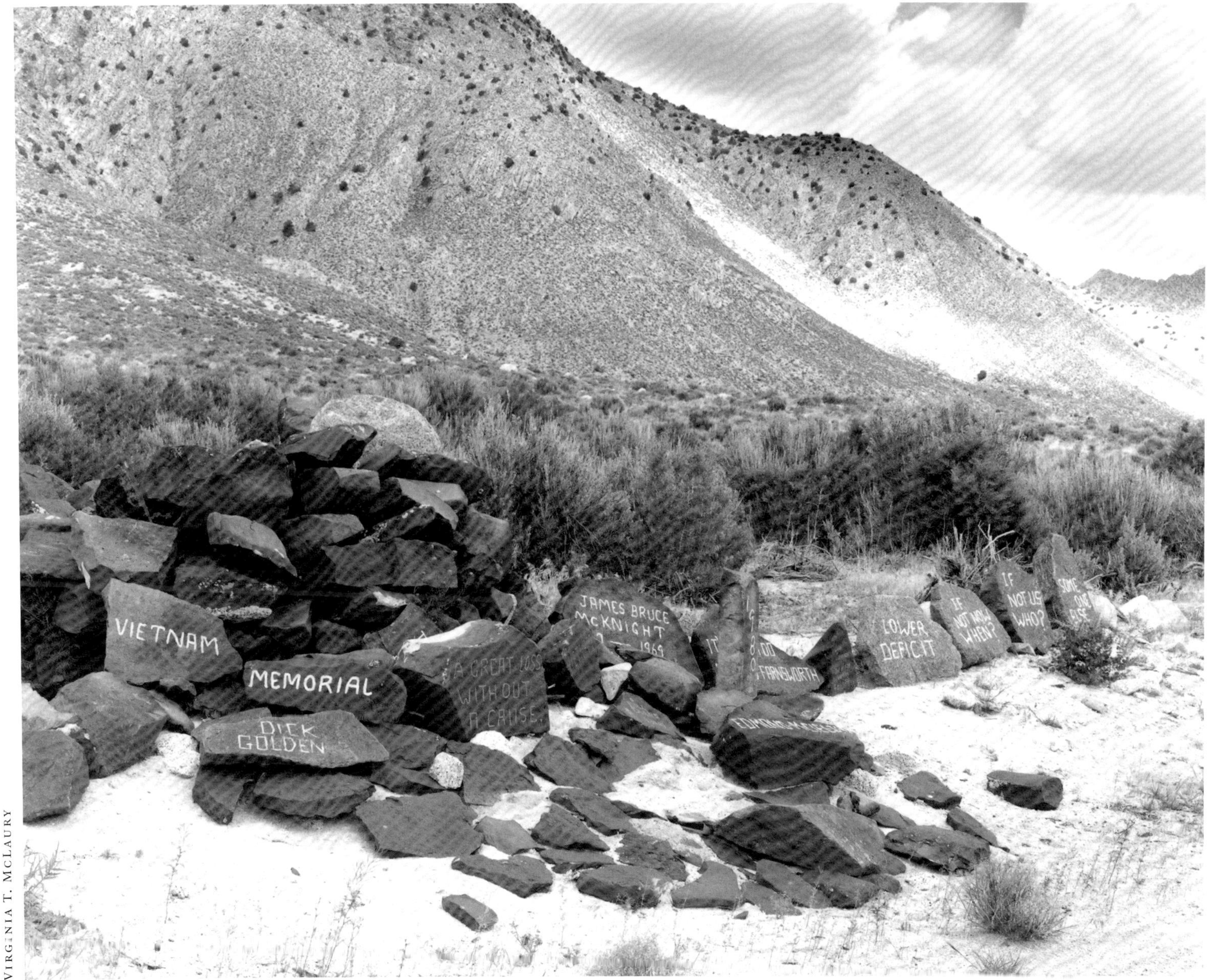
VIETNAM
MEMORIAL
DICK GOLDEN
JAMES BRUCE McKNIGHT
1969
A GREAT LOSS WITH OUT A CAUSE.
FARNSWORTH
LOWER DEFICIT
IF NOT NOW WHEN?
IF NOT US WHO?

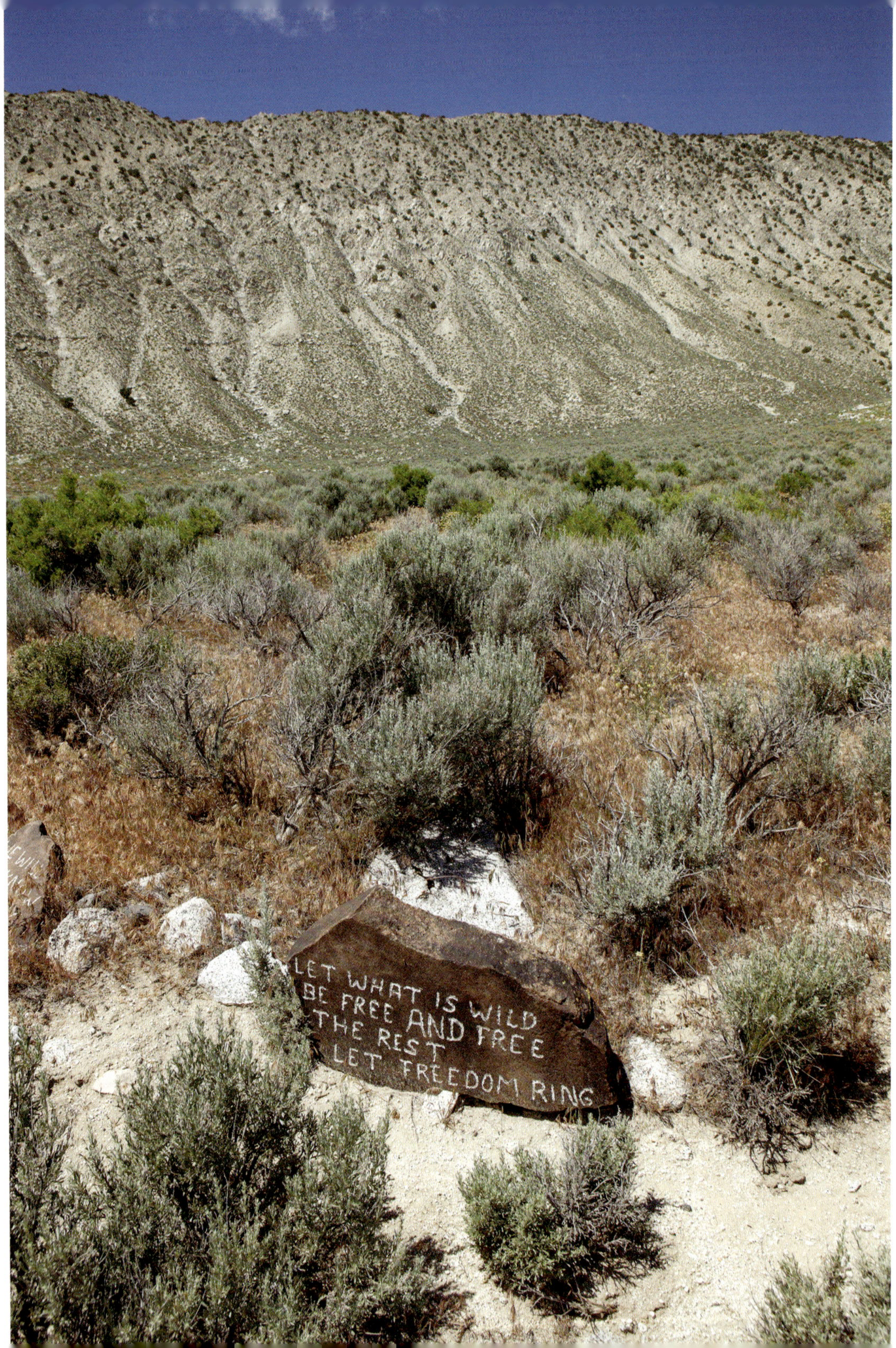
LET WHAT IS WILD
BE FREE AND FREE
THE REST
LET FREEDOM RING

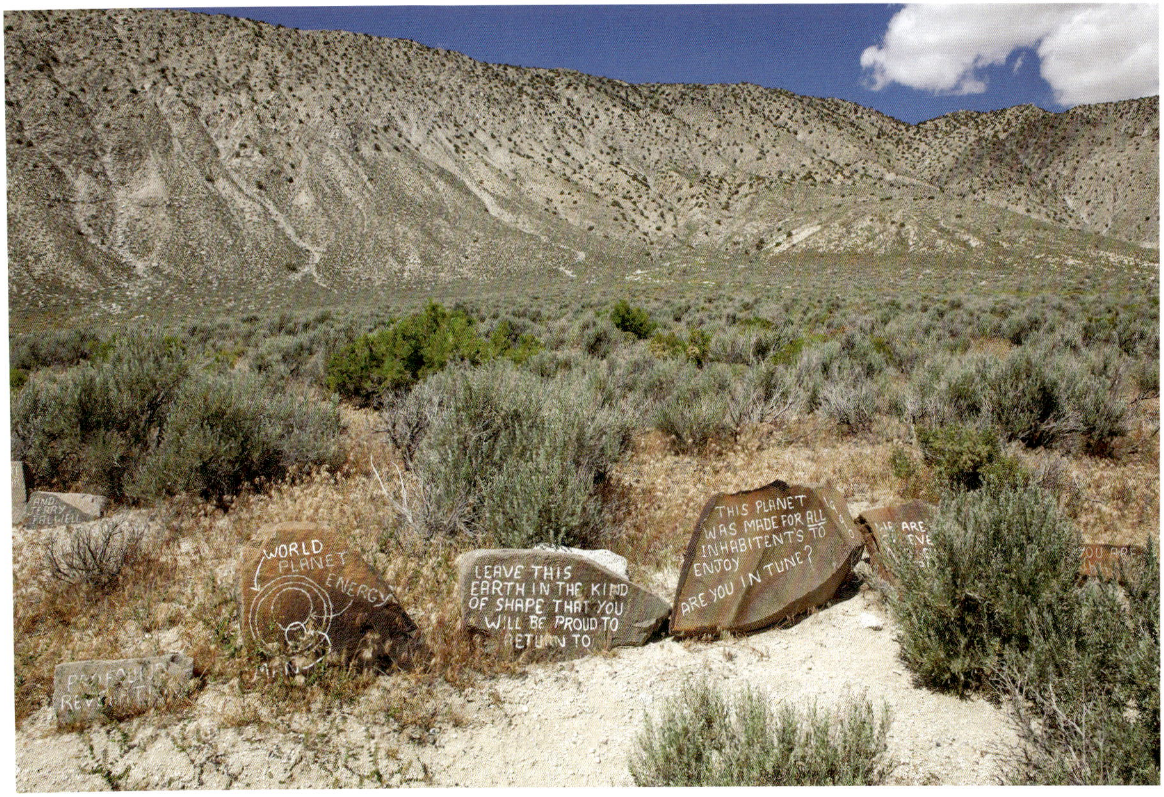
WORLD PLANET ENERGY
LEAVE THIS EARTH IN THE KIND OF SHAPE THAT YOU WILL BE PROUD TO RETURN TO
THIS PLANET WAS MADE FOR ALL INHABITENT'S TO ENJOY
ARE YOU IN TUNE?

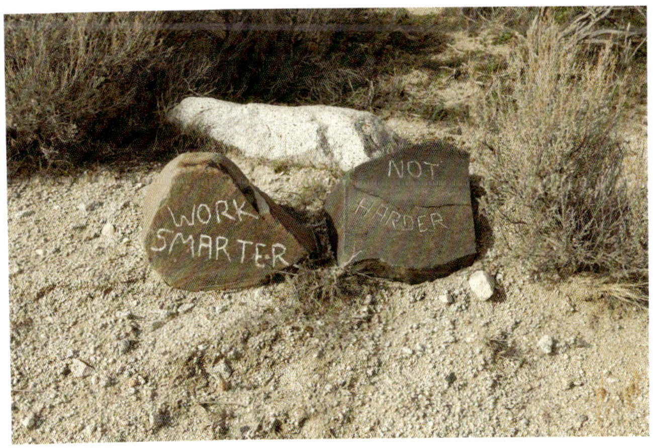
WORK SMARTER
NOT HARDER

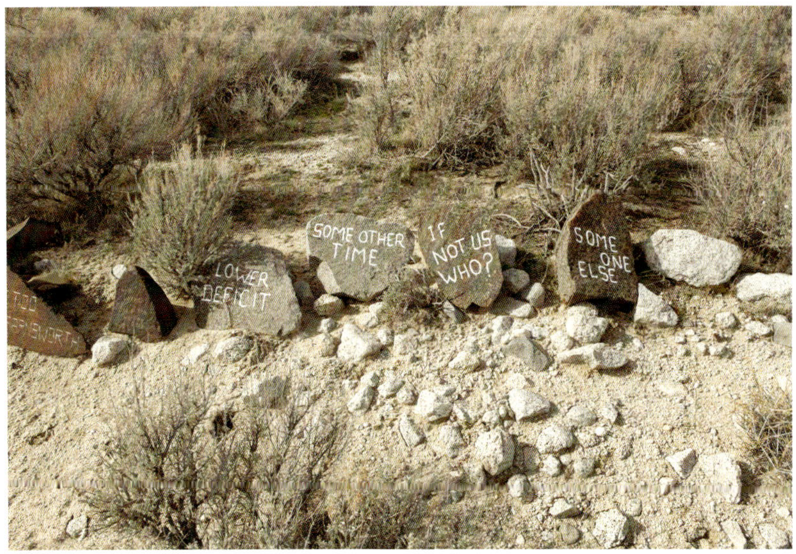
LOWER DEFICIT
SOME OTHER TIME
IF NOT US WHO?
SOME ONE ELSE

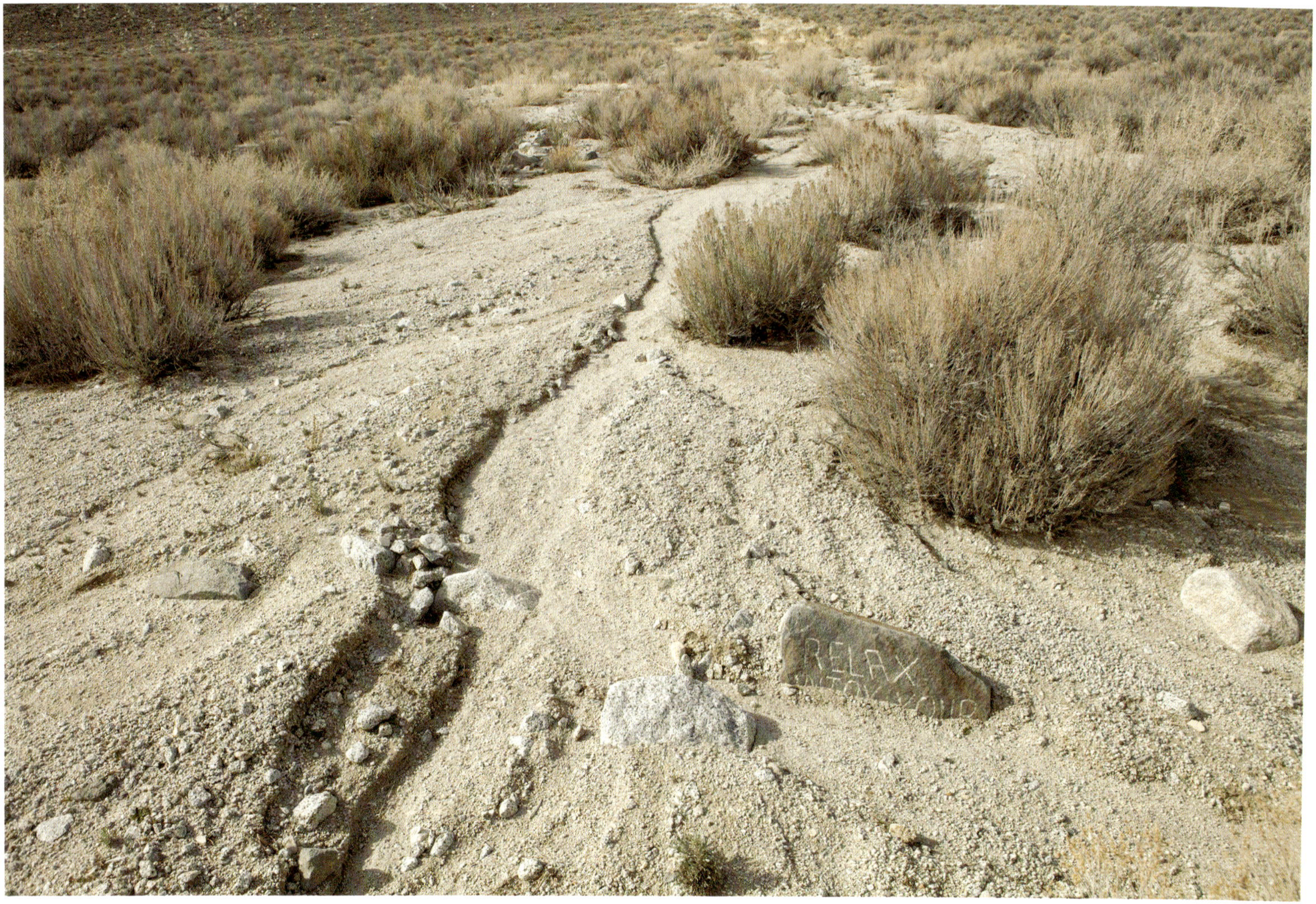
RELAX

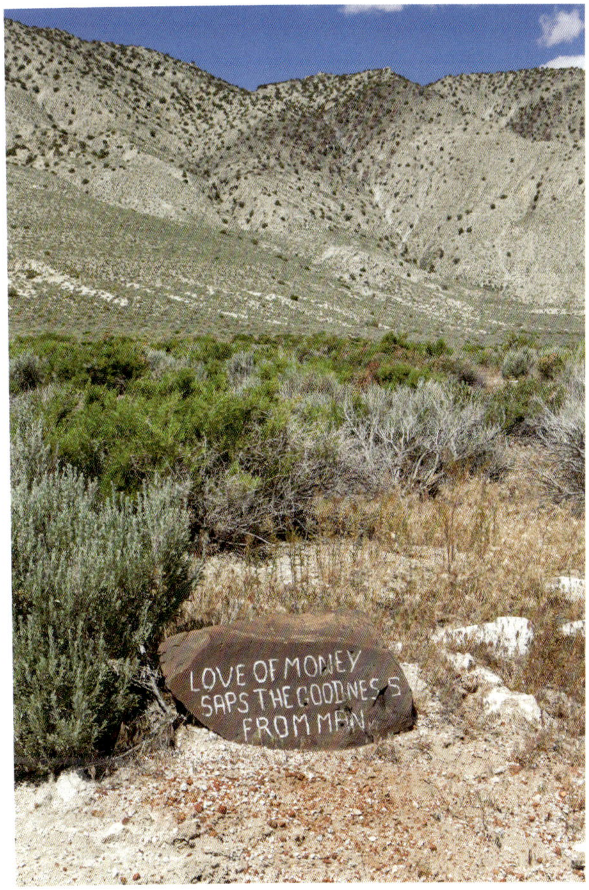
LOVE OF MONEY
SAPS THE GOODINESS
FROM MAN

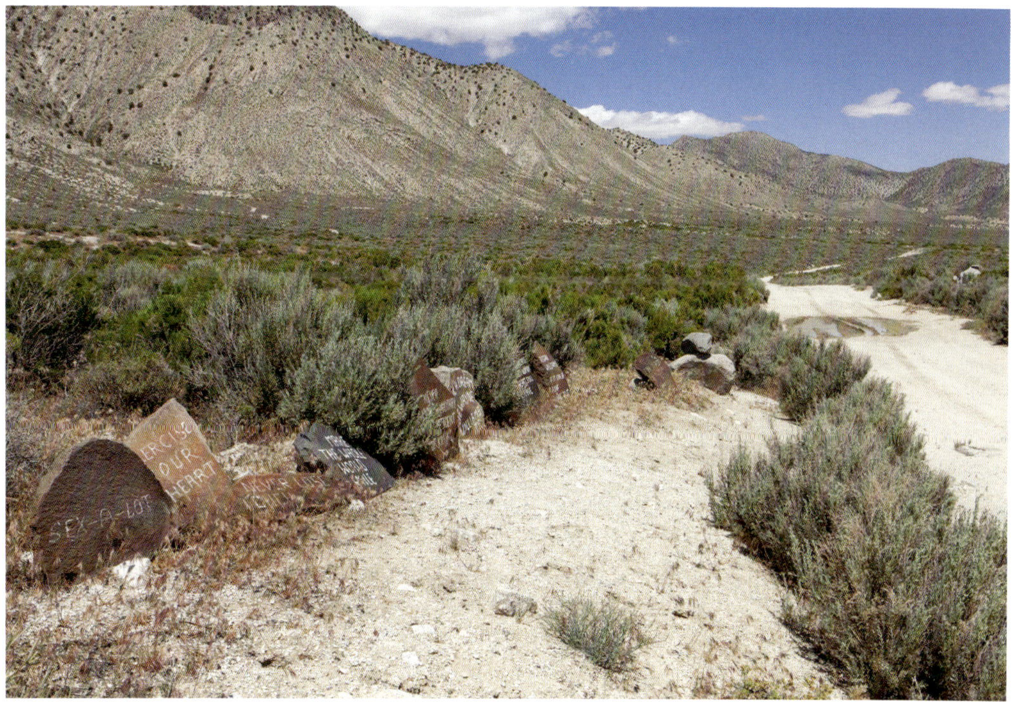
SEX-A-LOT
ERCISE
OUR
HEART

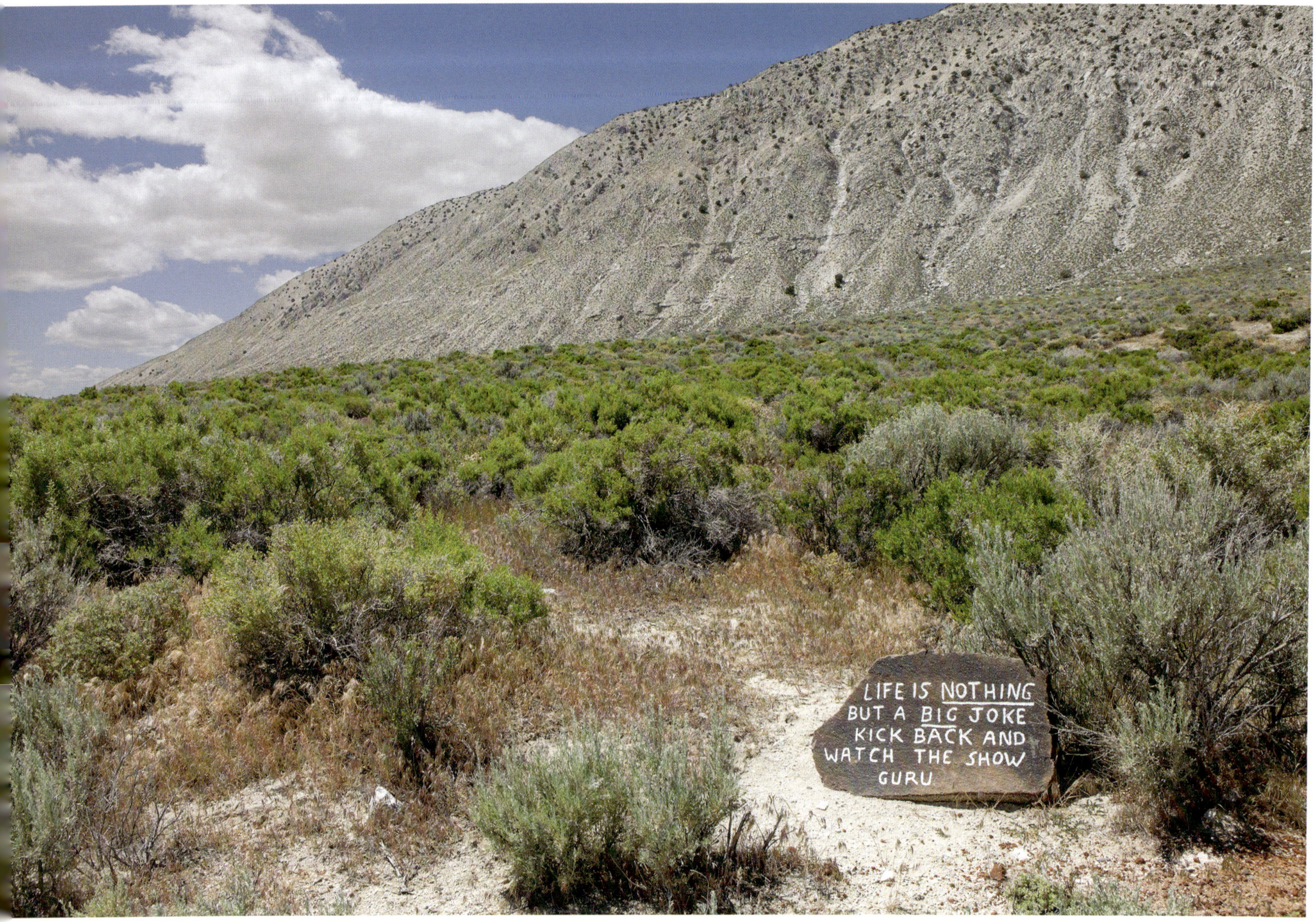
LIFE IS NOTHING
BUT A BIG JOKE
KICK BACK AND
WATCH THE SHOW
GURU

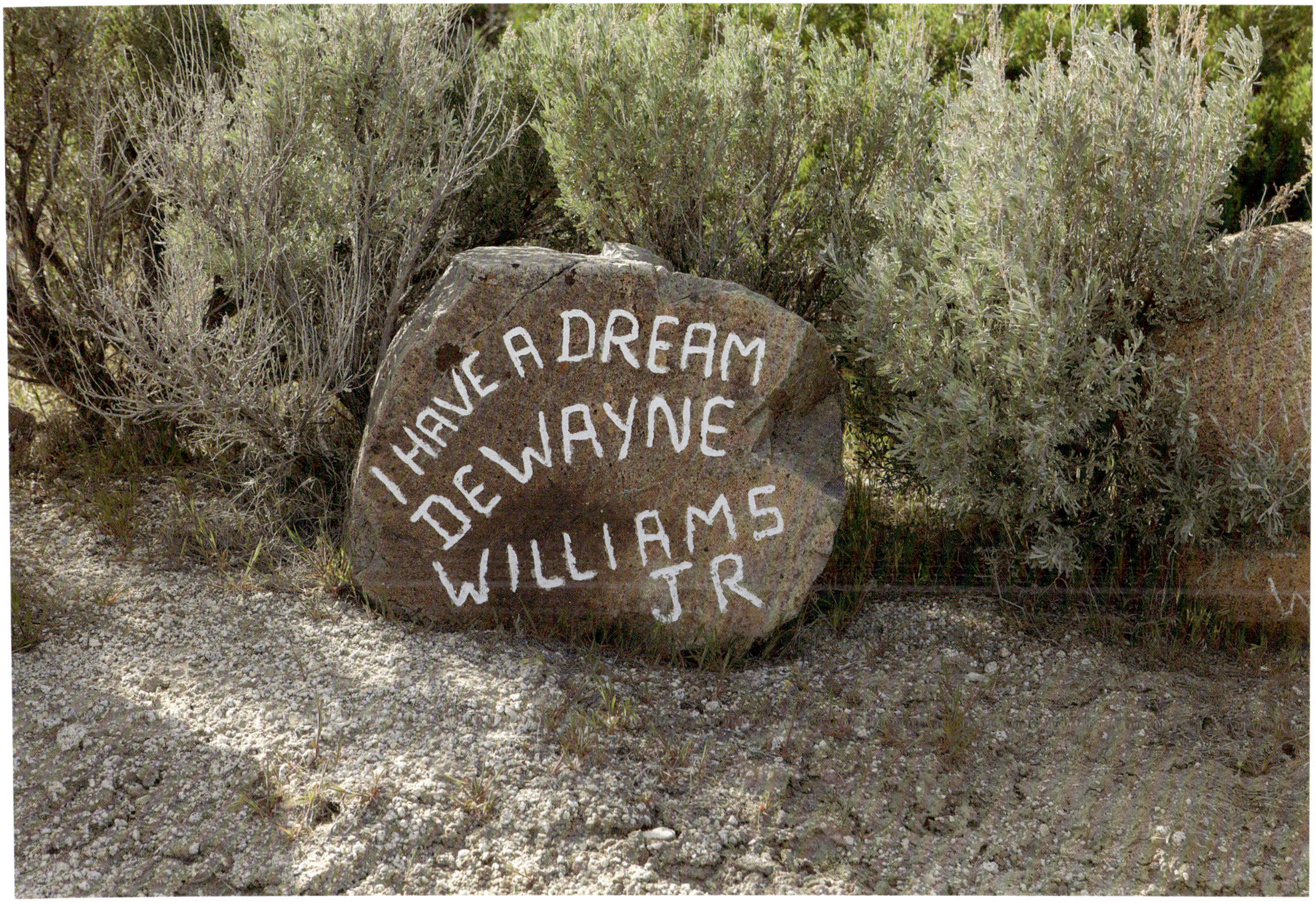
I HAVE A DREAM
DEWAYNE
WILLIAMS
JR

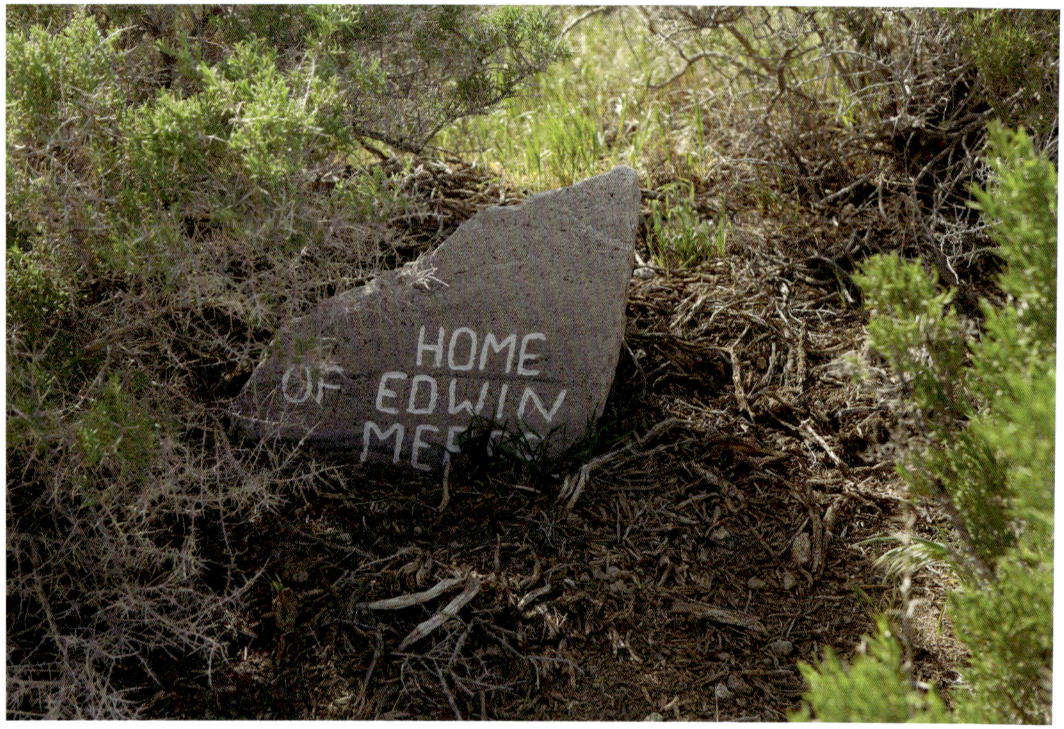
HOME
OF EDWIN

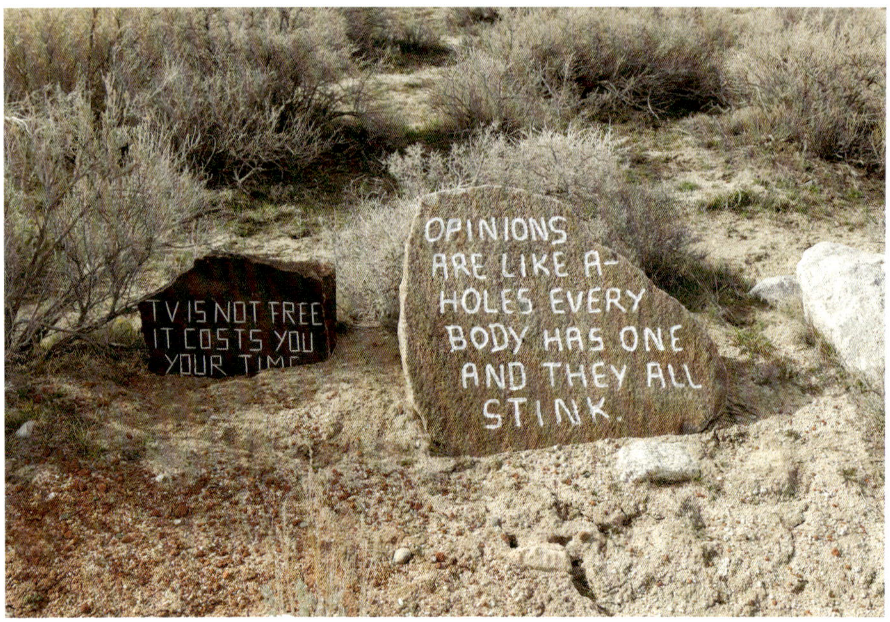
TV IS NOT FREE
IT COSTS YOU
OPINIONS
ARE LIKE A-
HOLES EVERY
BODY HAS ONE
AND THEY ALL
STINK.

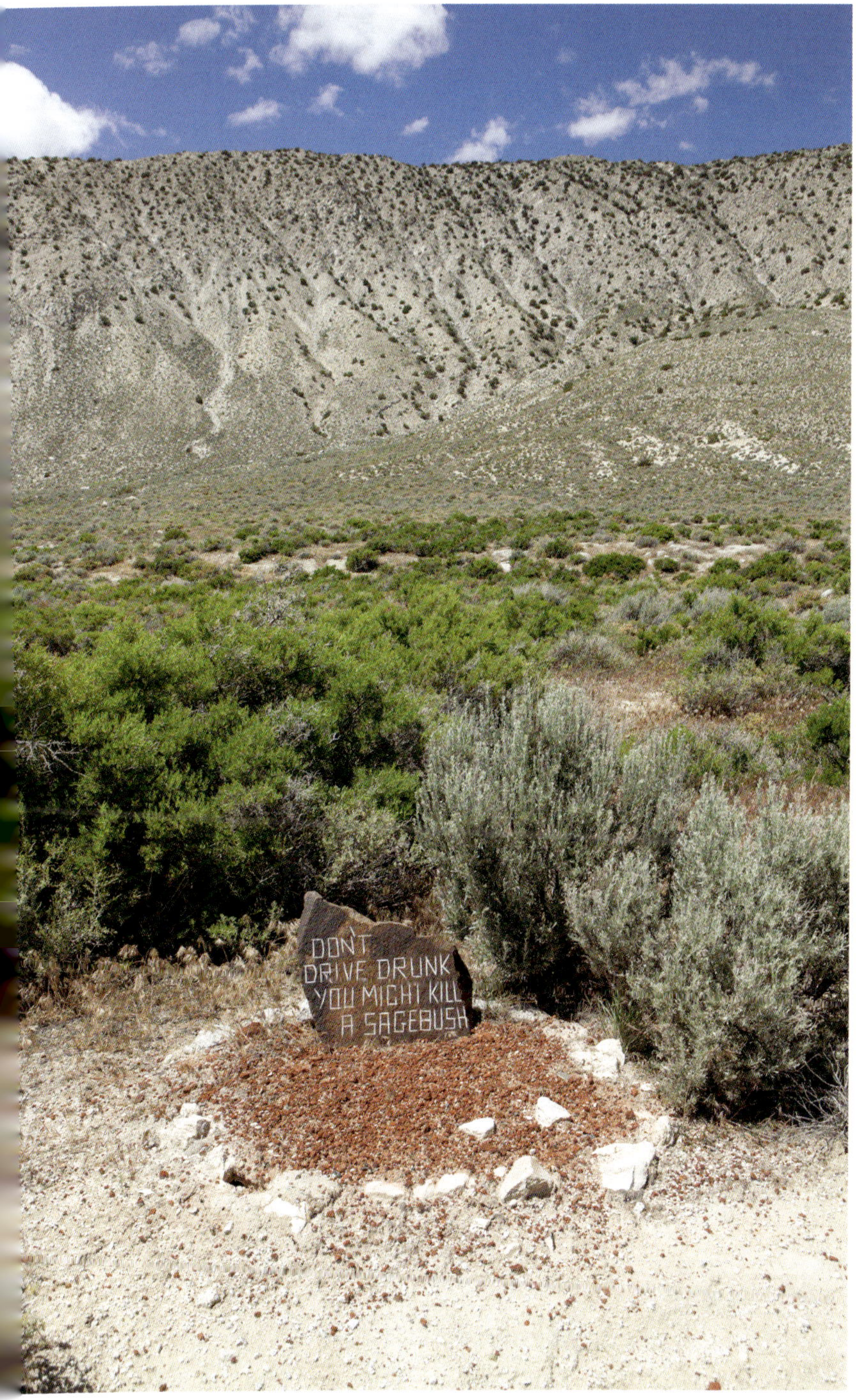
DON'T
DRIVE DRUNK
YOU MIGHT KILL
A SAGEBUSH

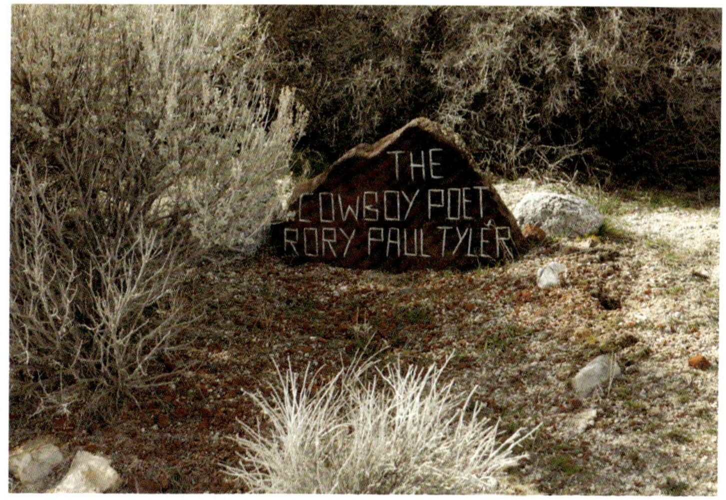
THE
COWBOY POET
RORY PAUL TYLER

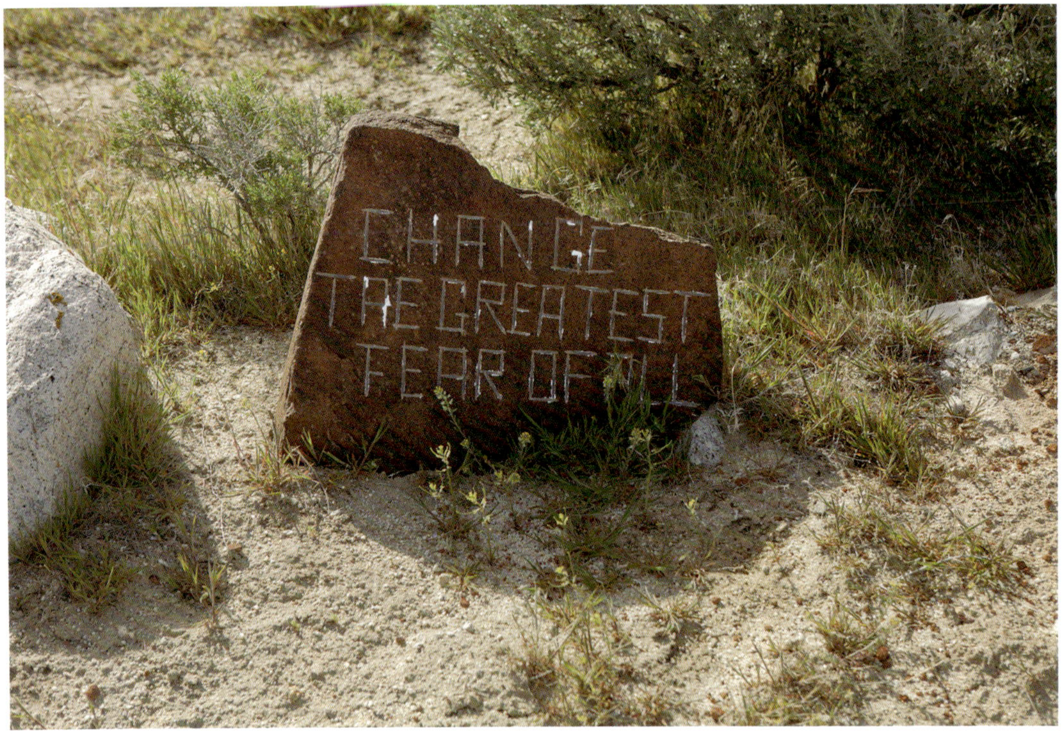
CHANGE
THE GREATEST
FEAR OF

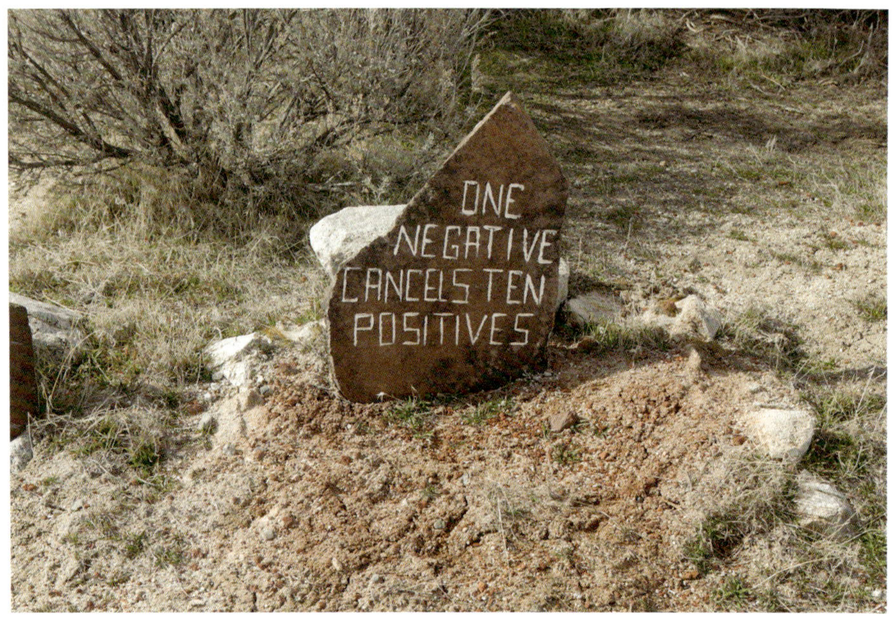
ONE
NEGATIVE
CANCELS TEN
POSITIVES

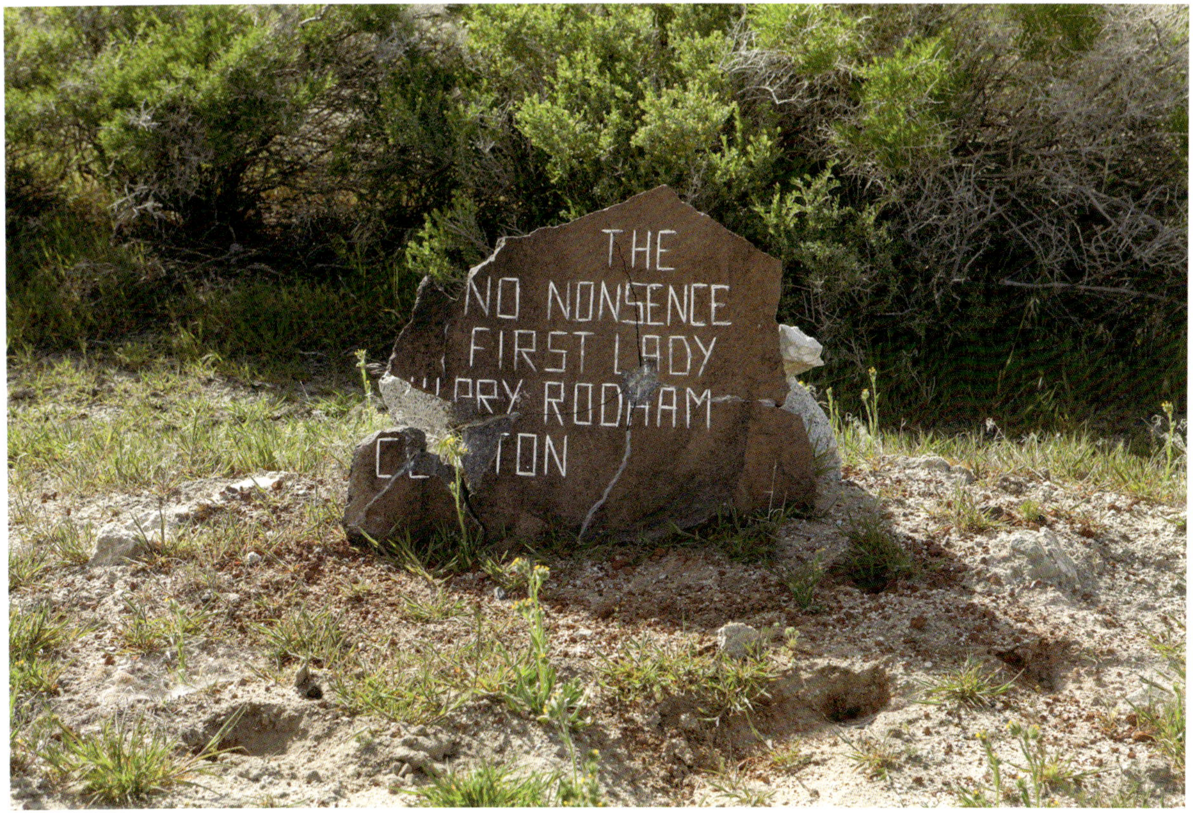
THE
NO NONSENCE
FIRST LADY
RODHAM

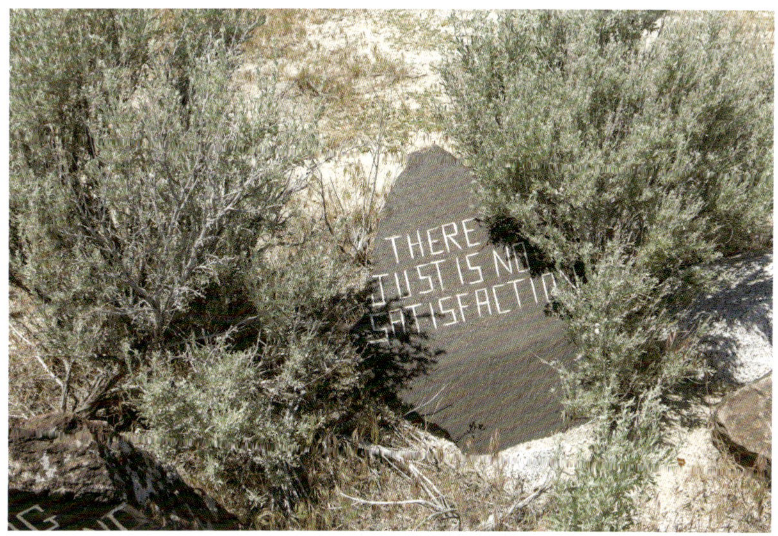
THERE
JUST IS NO

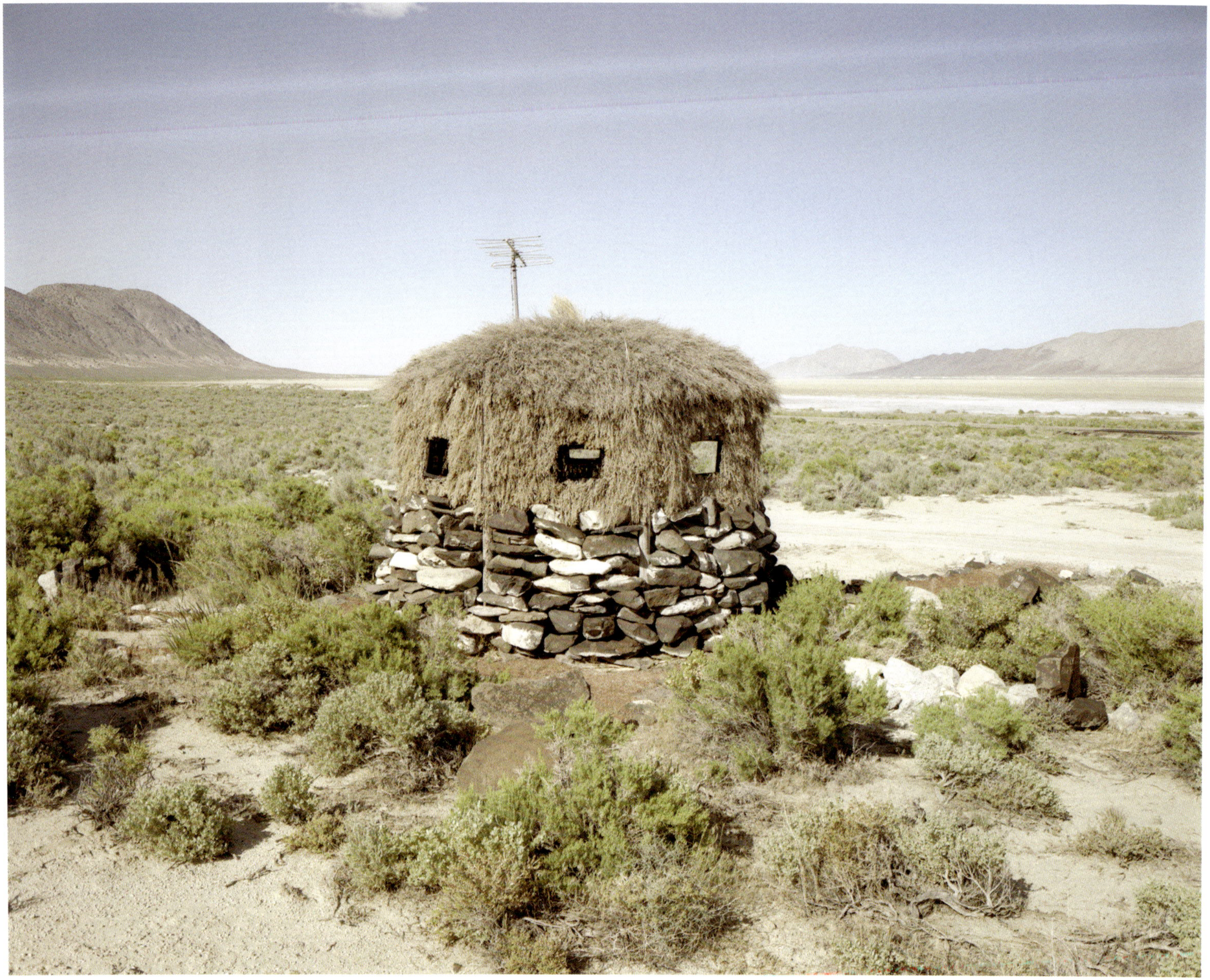

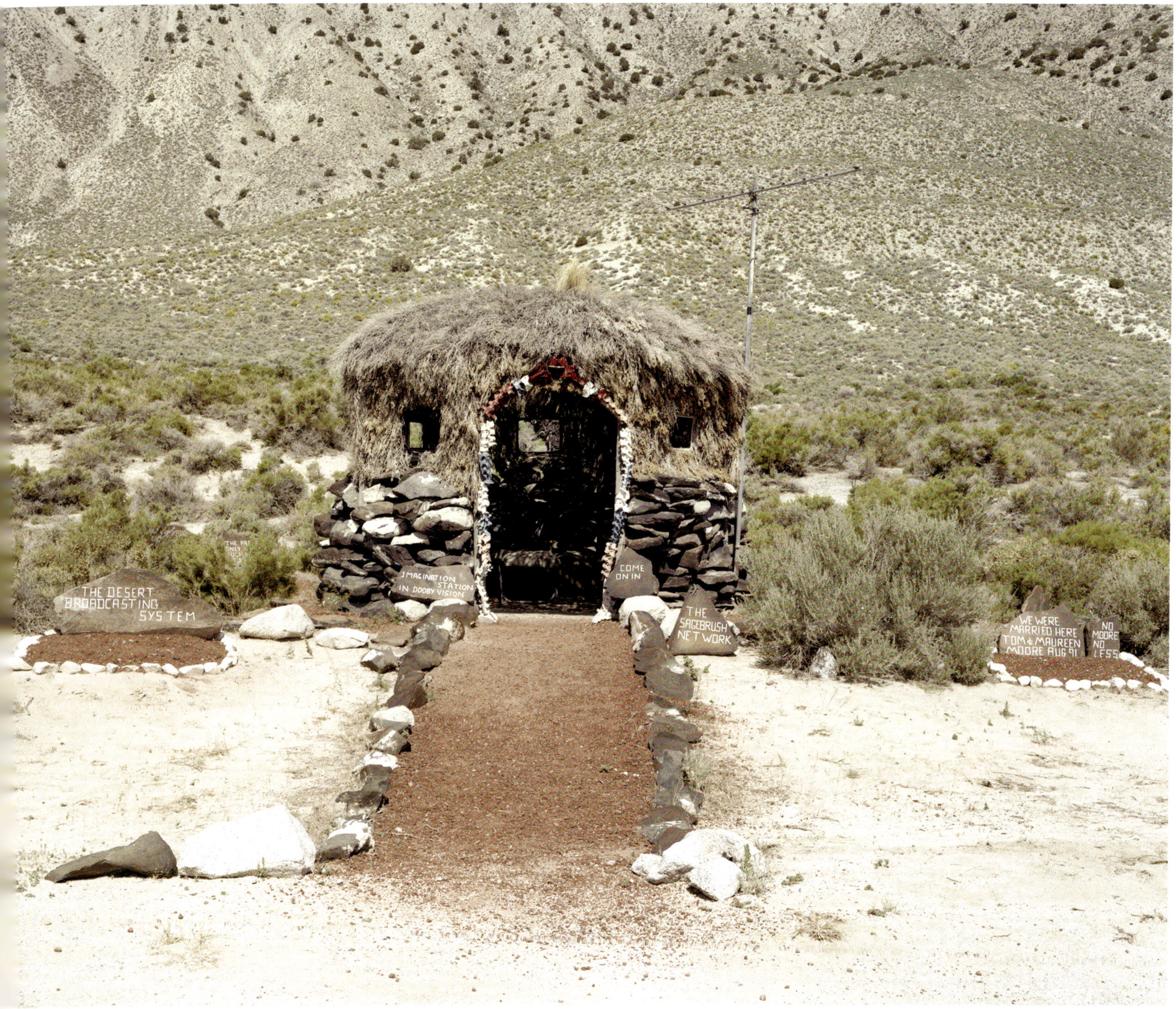
THE DESERT BROADCASTING SYSTEM
IMAGINATION STATION IN DOOBY VISION
COME ON IN
THE SAGEBRUSH NETWORK
WE WERE MARRIED HERE TOM & MAUREEN MOORE AUG 91
NO MOORE NO LESS

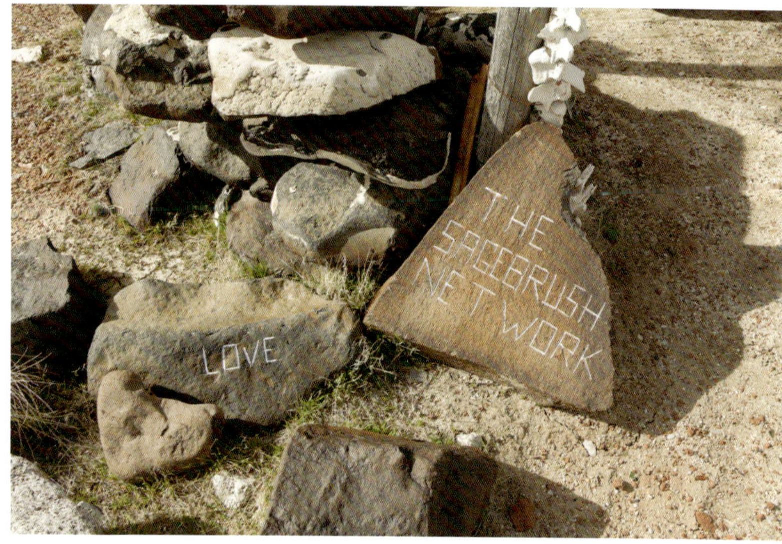
LOVE
THE
SAGEBRUSH
NETWORK

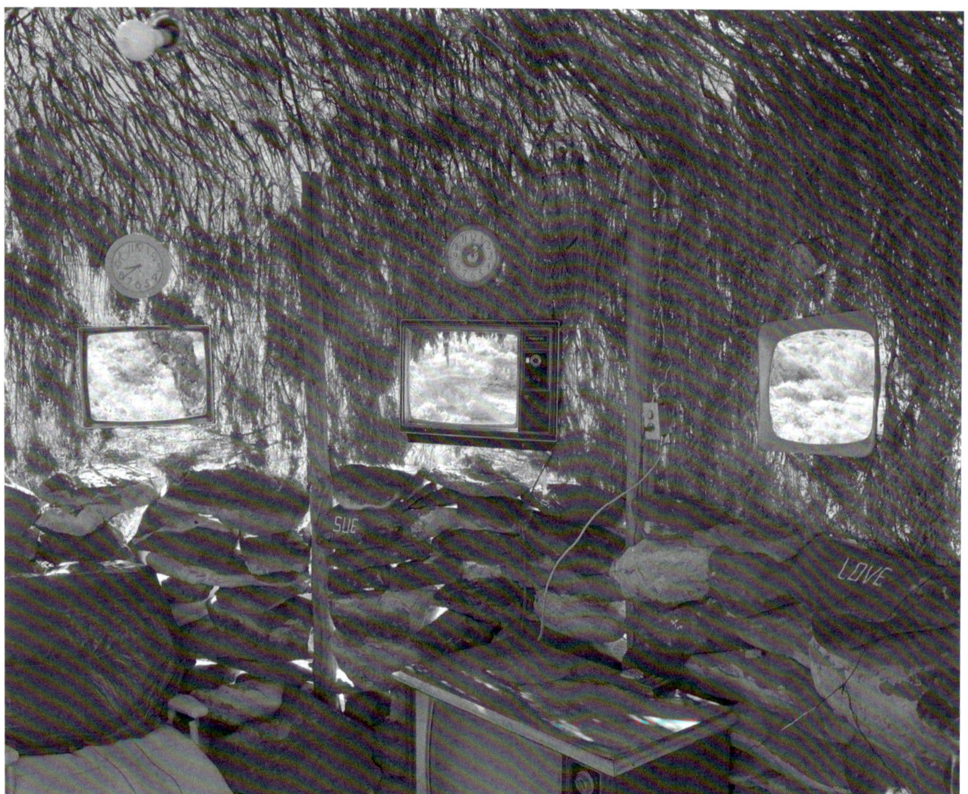
SUE
LOVE

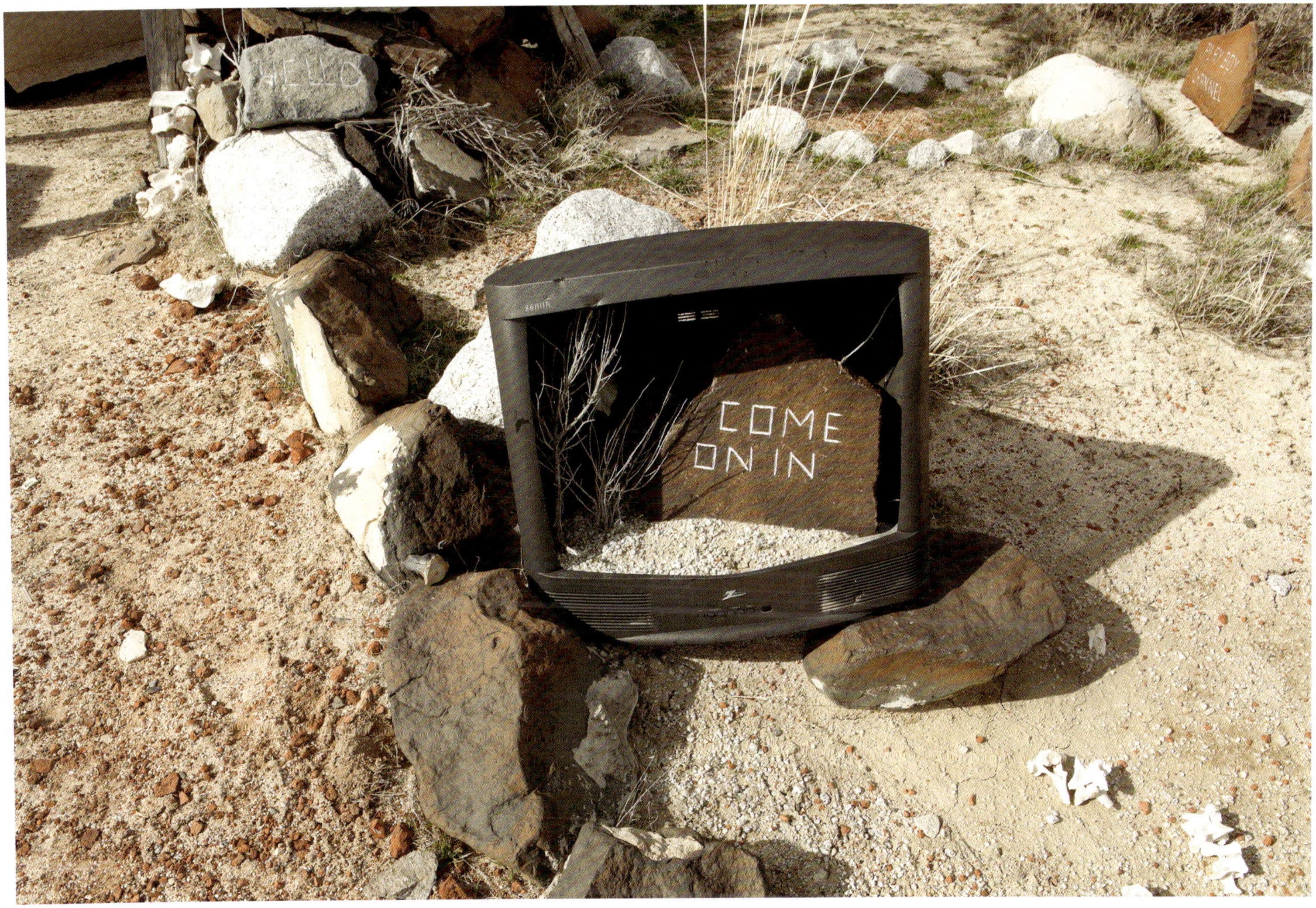
HELLO
COME
ON IN

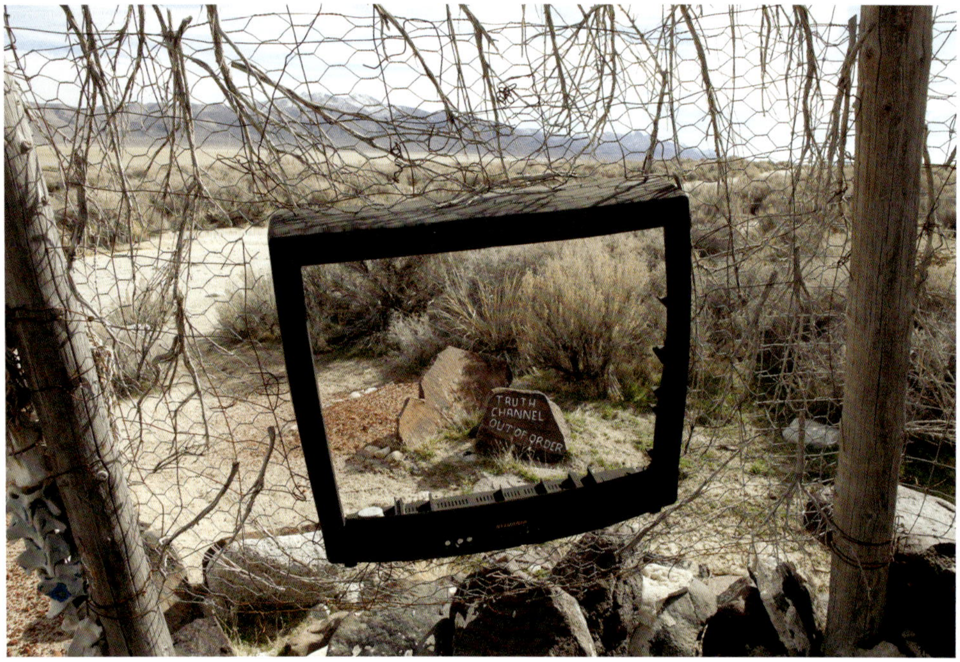
TRUTH
CHANNEL
OUT OF ORDER

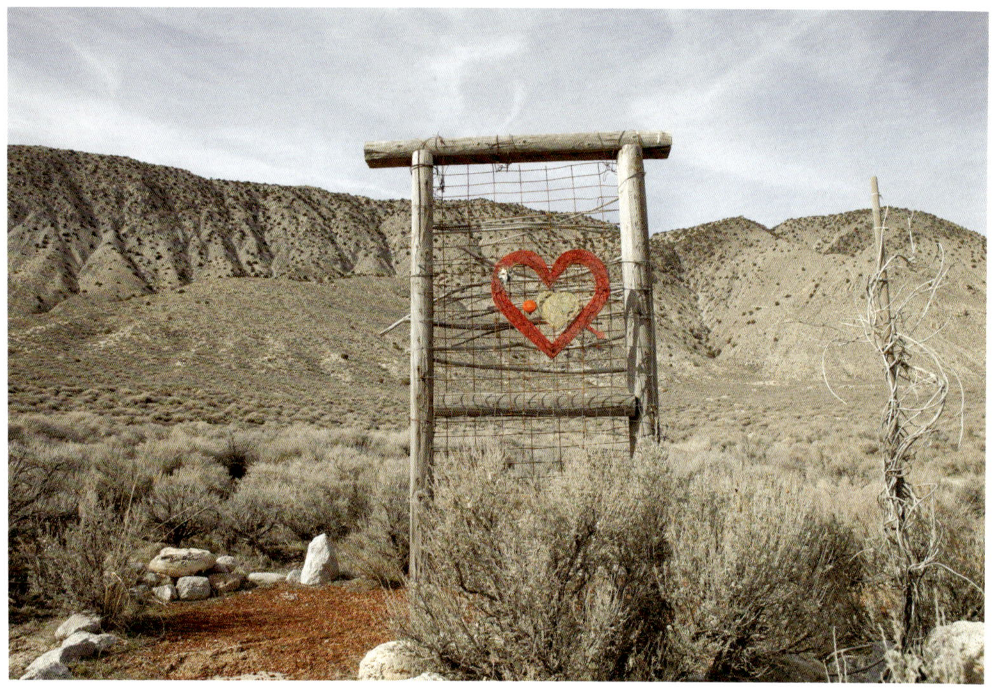

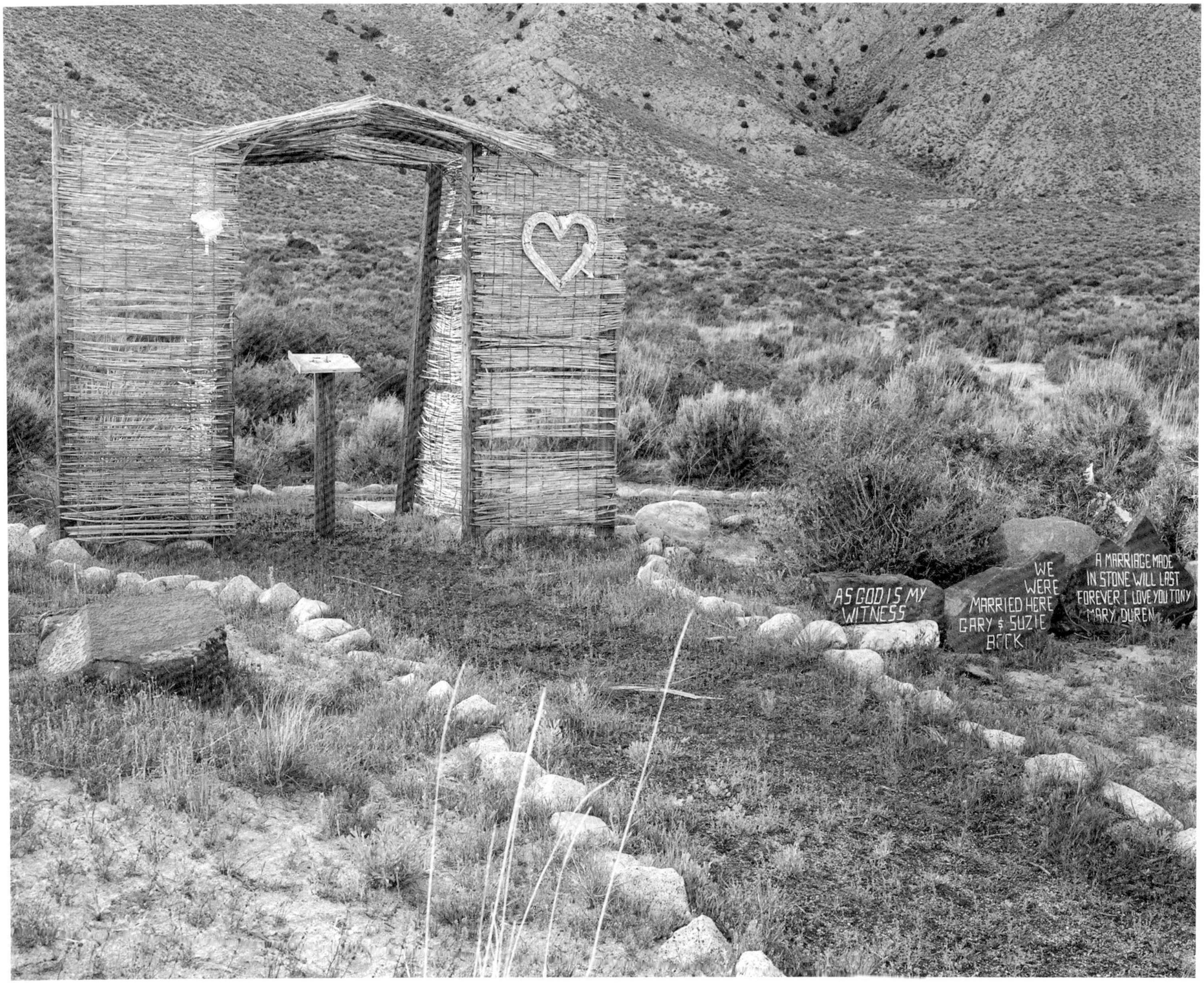
AS GOD IS MY WITNESS
WE WERE MARRIED HERE GARY & SUZIE
A MARRIAGE MADE IN STONE WILL LAST FOREVER I LOVE YOU TONY MARY DUREN

Afterword

BY GARY SNYDER

Carole and many neighbors and friends made trips to the Black Rock playa over subsequent years, and I always stopped and re-walked Guru Lane. I met DeWayne Williams right when he was working on a new installation — there were many. He knew I was a poet and a desert rat, and the two of us related as artists, with a certain distance and reserve — in our frayed and dusty jeans squinting in the sun. He told me of his cancer and a mysterious fungus that was coming from China to help him. Yet later, a few independent and sometimes clumsy installations that didn't last long were inserted by outsiders. DeWayne himself put in a "weather station" and stone chapel circle for couples getting married; as our society slowly slid onward downward he noted it with more dry funny comments.

A group of locals put themselves to looking after Guru Road, keeping it trash free and remaining DeWayne's own project. Then the remarkable unfolding of the annual Burning Man gathering began. Guru Road, close as it was to the entrance area for Burning Man, seemed almost invisible and was usually overlooked by the streams of cars that turned off the little highway and onto the trackless playa heading for a great emptiness "over there." I spent many nights and days out in the Black Rock including times when the Burning Man celebration was going full swing. Just drive ten more miles up the hardpan flat white playa and it all fades away, it cannot be seen or heard. Or, if it makes you feel better, go twenty miles. My friend the Japanese poet Shige stood there one night looking at the stars in the sky with a tear in his eye saying, "I never knew there were so many." When I let my new dog out at daylight, she looked totally baffled by being surrounded by no phenomena at all.

It was DeWayne's gift to make his circle of friends and family in Gerlach become "the stars in the sky" and put us all into the same universe, using just the roadside rocks, and never a mean word.

put a chain around it. We took off, and that tree flew right out of the ground by the roots . . . and we drove it in here, dug a hole, [and] Dan threw a great big boulder on the roots, and everything. I shoveled the dirt back in there, and we came back in three weeks later and the tree was growin' and I thought goddamn. I can't believe that, I felt so bad for pulling out a live tree. I was goin' to put a rock up on there that says THE LAST OF NEVADA'S GREAT FORCE *. . . and then I thought, well gee, might get lonely out here by itself. So I planted another to keep it company. And I come out every week and water them. And fertilize it and the rats eat it.*

One day I came out here and there were two, three, beautiful ladies. All sittin' on that rock out there. And I got to know 'em. We talked, and they finally had to go back home, it was Sunday night and then they showed up again. They came up to see their boyfriend and the boyfriend was in Winnemucca at that time, so they said, "Hell, Dooby, will ya' show us around?" Hell yeah, Christ, couldn't pass up a chance like that, these three lovely ladies. So I took 'em way up in the mountains and showed them some antelope, wild horses, and they said, ". . . are there any hot pools?". . . The only ones I knew [that] were open we had to cross the desert. I said I know some over there. "Okay let's go over to the hot pool," and we went over to the hot pools and they stripped off all their clothes and got in the damn water and was bathin' and having the biggest time, man, it was like goin' to the show, shit, it was like a movie I didn't have to pay nothing for. And I love those girls, they're great. And I put two flowers in the desert. They are beautiful ladies. They don't eat meat. They don't drink. They don't smoke, they don't do nothing. I don't know how in the hell they live.

. . . And that damn Indian revenge. You see what happened there? We come over here and take up the damn land and what do they do, they say we'll get even with you bastards, and they gave us tobacco. And what did we do? We smoked them bastards, I even chew, even now.

This is my commandment: If we could stomp out grief, wipe out envy, and never assume, never. You just think of the times you've assumed and how many times you've been wrong. Believe only what can be proved. Keep smiling, think health, drink milk, sex-a-lot, exercise your heart.

DeWayne Williams breathed his last breath on January 11, 1995.

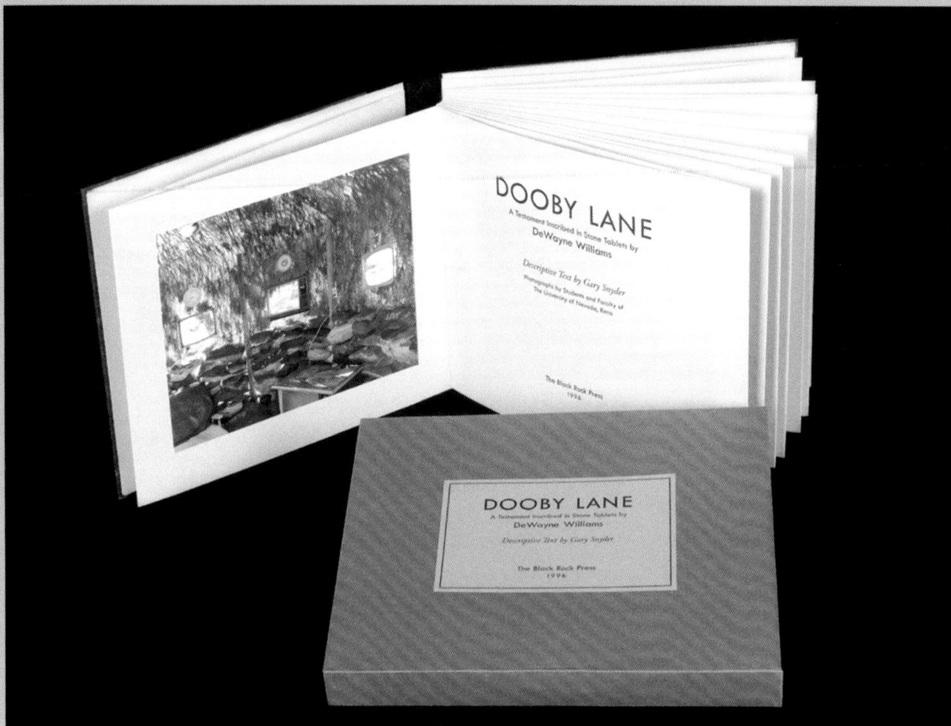

While traveling the high arid regions of northern Nevada in 1988, Gary Snyder and his wife, Carole, happened upon Dooby Lane, outside Gerlach, on the edge of the vast and flat playa of the Black Rock Desert. Known also as Guru Road and Doobie Avenue, Dooby Lane is a mile-long collection of inscriptions on stone and found-object assemblages that display the musing, imagination, and hard work of DeWayne Williams, longtime citizen of Gerlach, Nevada, and the Cosmos. Surprised and immediately captivated by the wisdom and humor of the work, Gary decided to write down a detailed description of his discovery. The result is included in the first iteration of Dooby Lane, *an accordion-fold limited-edition artist book published by the Black Rock Press under the guidance of John Balkwill, master printer, and Peter Goin, photographer and Foundation Professor of Art.*

Photographer's Notes

BY PETER GOIN

The idea of the accordion-fold book originated in the fall of 1995. Gary, who had learned of DeWayne's passing earlier in the year, sent a copy of the notes he had written in 1988 with the suggestion it would make sense for a fine art letterpress publisher named after the Black Rock to do a book on one of the desert's most remarkable sites. Gary wanted Dooby Lane to gain the wider recognition it deserves as a unique, creative work. He also hoped people might start thinking of ways to protect the site, if not from the corroding effects of time, at least from the destructive acts of careless people.

Creating a book on Dooby Lane seemed like the perfect opportunity to combine text with photographic images. John Balkwill and I share common interests, and we had been thinking of ways to work collaboratively. What resulted was the idea for a unique fieldwork and letterpress workshop in which advanced photography students participated in the project from photographing to binding. What resulted was a hand-made accordion-fold edition of 50 copies reflecting many hours of hard work by eight enthusiastic, highly skilled, and diligent students from the University of Nevada, Reno. The students — *Irene Kung, Chanda Beck, Lara K. Schott, Amy Chatowski, Stacey Wittek, Virginia T. McLaury, Christina Spielvogel*, and *Suzy Kelley* — spent nearly a week in May 1996 field camping in a spectacular grove of trees north of the Leadville mining site.

Under my supervision, this advanced photography field workshop photographed Dooby Lane using large-format field cameras and Kodak Tri-X black-and-white negative film. Once the fieldwork was completed, the students and I returned to the photography studios and laboratory and spent more than eight days carefully processing the negatives and printing archivally on Ilford gelatin silver photographic paper.

Starting on the following Monday, the students spent two weeks at the Black Rock Press doing the homework and training involved in the construction of the book. Once the pages were printed, the original photographs were tipped into the accordion-fold volume according to exacting standards. The fine art accordion-fold books sold out almost immediately, and only a few people were able to view the books thereafter.

Time passes, but neither Gary nor I gave up the idea of printing a trade edition of *Dooby Lane*. Basically, the idea was simply to update the book and make it more accessible to a wider audience. Jack Shoemaker, editorial director and vice-president at Counterpoint Press in Berkeley, California, met with me in fall 2015. At his urging, I submitted a proposal that formed the basis for this book, although what I discovered in my subsequent research was a treasure trove of new information. Recording all the names, or at least a majority of the names carved into the stone tablets, took nearly a full day. The nearly 300 names did not include those names buried or abandoned, removed or stolen. What others have absconded with creates an absence that could only through tireless research be recovered. That is the fundamental fact of Dooby Lane — it changes over time as people interact with the site, moving rocks from there to here, or introducing rejected stones back into the limelight, or adding detritus that has no relationship to DeWayne Williams's creative urges. The occasional microbursts flush the hillsides descending from the Granite Range, eviscerating everything in the way of the mud, water, and boulders. There are, undoubtedly, numerous carved tablets now buried under the roadway, or farther below towards Highway 34. While conducting our accounting and recording, my assistant and I uncovered a couple of tablets and returned them to a rightful place along the promenade.

The names reveal a chronicle of Gerlach through the mind's eye of DeWayne Williams. Dooby Lane is an enduring narrative that while requiring restoration and maintenance has as its foundation the etched stones, permanent unto themselves. These stones, and the names placed upon them, list the people who populated Gerlach and bring the town's human history to a form of poetic resonance. The geneology of Dooby Lane is an ongoing process of discovery as each name has its own history, relationships, perspectives, and role in the overall chronicle.

Dooby Lane is organized sequentially, more or less from the entrance to Guru Road to its exit, a mile-plus in the distance. Since there are more than 450 stone tablets, not all of them could be reproduced, but the names available to my team in the winter and spring of 2016 are listed, alphabetically. The annotations are a beginning, not a conclusive or reductionist list of identifiers, but, instead, a series of portals, introductions to the many stories untold. Originally, my photographic work at Dooby Lane was exposed using a Horseman 4x5 field camera, but since the revolution in digital technologies, the majority of photographs in this book employ digital formats, mostly from a Canon EOS 5D camera.

The final product of this work will be a publicly accessible collection of photographs, documents, videotapes, voice recordings, and the original journals left in the mailbox. The tablet says THANKS FOR THE COMMENTS. This collection can be supplemented with the audience's photographs, memorabilia, and videos, should there be sufficient interest in building the memorial. The experience is well worth it, but a traveler needs to know where to go and how to get there. As DeWayne Williams said, "If you don't have a guide, you can't get to the promise land. See the guru's got to be the guide."

The Dooby Lane Collection will reside in Special Collections, University of Nevada, Reno Libraries.

Restoring the Road

BY MICHAEL MYERS
Executive Director, Friends of Black Rock-High Rock

Friends of Black Rock-High Rock was formed in 1999 to help manage the resources of the Black Rock Desert. The Friends' core mission involves educating the public and fostering stewardship in an effort to preserve the region's unique character. The Friends is essentially a volunteer organization; most of the projects focus on involving those willing to donate their time and energy into restoring, preserving, and protecting the Black Rock landscape. Other activities include a more formal role within the local school and assisting or providing information, brochures, maps, books, and other materials to those stopping by the Friends' visitor center in Gerlach. The Friends conduct outreach events spreading the word of the Black Rock Desert at events such as Earth Day. The Friends sponsors an Artist-in-Residence program, serves as a Wild & Scenic Film Festival on Tour host site, and is leading the way in an ongoing effort to restore Dooby Lane.

Dooby Lane encapsulates and represents a multitude of meanings since many visitors know little of Gerlach or its community of citizens. Many of the sayings on the rocks are tributes to those who live or lived in Gerlach. Oftentimes a phrase is an inside joke between the person being recognized and DeWayne Williams, or Dooby. Some of the phrases are personal or political musings about the state of society. Others are more contemplative and philosophical in nature. The Friends have met with the citizens of Gerlach, visitors from out of the area, government officials, and with a few artists in order to determine the best course of action to preserve this unique art installation.

The art exhibits can be taken at face value, or the meaning might be more personalized or enigmatic. Upon further introspection, the sculptures and tablets may evoke very deep and personal meanings and connections. While the entirety of the road has the power to evoke strong emotions, it's true that some people come away unimpressed. A large majority of visitors enjoy the concept of such an odd, quirky art exhibit in the middle of a distant desert. However, countless people have spent considerable amount of time walking or driving Dooby Lane, reflecting, contemplating, and connecting with the exhibits, nature, and themselves. One of the goals of the Friends is to facilitate new visitors' experience at Dooby Lane, and to do so such that the avenue is in a similar state as when it was created. Dooby, Dan Deveny, and Dee Williams (DeWayne's son) were the principle team that created this art installation, and the Friends want to preserve it for future generations.

Nature in the Nevada desert is an unforgiving environment, especially for human-made installations and ephemeral structures. Dooby Lane has suffered from vandals, misanthropes, and the vagaries of weather. There is the view that part of the beauty of outdoor art installations is to witness them deteriorate over time. However, the Friends believe that Dooby Lane should be preserved. The restoration continues, although sporadically at best, due to limited resources.

The Friends' members come from a variety of backgrounds, and they have a multitude of interests and reasons for being involved in the organization. These include rock hounding, visiting the area's plethora of hot springs, tracking emigrant trail history, ranching, birding, hiking, camping, rocketry, photography, archaeology, and participating in the annual Burning Man festival. In some ways, the Friends is a liaison between the general public and the Bureau of Land Management, the federal agency responsible for overseeing much of Black Rock country. The Friends occasionally serves as an intermediary between the public and Burning Man, fulfilling a perceived gap in services as 70,000 or more people descend on the playa.

Reflecting their memory and connection to Dooby Lane, many of the same people keep coming back to help restore the road. Periodically, citizens of Gerlach will take it upon themselves to preserve sections or individual stone tablets. At least one outside group of citizens (Iron Butt) received permission from Dooby to create their own tribute to fallen members of their group. Throughout the year, people can be found touching up art exhibits, removing weeds or trash from the road, or generally caring for and loving this special place.

After DeWayne Williams's death in 1995, Dooby Lane began to fall into disrepair. The first major restoration project occurred in 2003. That year, Dooby's son Dee, the Friends' volunteers, and members of Burning Man's Department of Public Works (DPW) crew led by Matthew "Metric" Ebert collaborated and committed to restoring and rehabilitating some of the degraded sections of Dooby Lane. "Metric" later became the Executive Director of the Friends, and he was an influential force in ongoing restoration work.

Since 2003 and through 2011, the Friends have conducted volunteer restoration projects along Dooby Lane. During the 2003 effort, there were 27 volunteers. These projects have varied in scope and scale. In 2005, a rock-slide from a micro-burst along the front of the Granite Range washed away and buried many etched tablets, damaged portions of the road, and destabilized a few art sculptures and monuments. The Friends were able to clear the road and locate a few but not all of the washed-away tablets. Based on personal recollection and the significant photographic evidence in part provided by the author of this book, many tablets were returned to more or less the original location. Work to remove vegetation has been completed at "Ground Zero." The tablets at "Ground Zero" were moved closer to their original locations. At one point, the Aphrodite sculpture was targeted to stabilize the structure and to restore its original appearance. The "Comments" mailbox had to be rebuilt after it collapsed. Volunteers pulled weeds, making it much easier for visitors to view the writing on the tablets. Volunteers also painted some of the letters with white paint, making them easier to read/view. "The Sagebrush Network" TV station was in serious disrepair. The thatch-like roof was reconstructed, and the art installment was solidified in an upright position. The "Leave Your Hang Ups Here" tepee had fallen into disrepair and was also reconstructed. Although many people have made conscious decisions to add specific objects to the tepee, the structure has been saddled with trash and garbage. The Friends have thoughtfully removed objects that are clearly trash and not a part of the overall structure. This can be a sensitive topic, so, for the most part, the exhibit is left in its evolved state. But, at the same time, the Friends would like to prevent objects that have fallen from blowing away and becoming trash out on the landscape. During one of the earlier restoration projects, graffiti had to be scrubbed off some of the rocks. Portions of the road have been reconstructed and rehabilitated to help reduce further erosion. This is an ongoing battle between human access and the weather.

Elvis's cape was a specific restoration effort within the overall project. Dooby's son Dee spent many hours crafting a cape from 1,200 aluminum can bases. They were intricately woven together so that they would shimmer in the sun, and in a windy environment, the rattling of the can cape makes its own form of music. The Friends continue hosting volunteer projects that are designed to help preserve Dooby Lane for current and future generations. The Friends are proud to play a role in keeping alive this piece of art and history. For further information, contact the Friends at blackrockdesert.org. Long live Dooby Lane!

Names

List of names etched into stone tablets as recorded by Stephen Davis, February 23, 2016. Annotated by Judy Conley, Ardyss Williams, Dee Williams, Dan Deveny, and Peter Goin.

This list of tablets includes some but not all of the names that were added after DeWayne Williams's death. Based upon the style and character of the etched names, some of the post-Williams tablets are easily identified, others less so. Some names are present at the north end of the avenue and include deceased former Gerlach residents. Where a number is indicated parenthetically, it indicates that the name was on that number of stones. If the number is in bold, that indicates that the number was included on the stone.

A

Erica Adams Alumnus of Gerlach High School (1997–2001).

Joe and **Teresa Adams** Joe and Teresa Adams were neighbors of DeWayne Williams. Erica, Joey, Mike, Nick, and Tracy were their children.

Joey Adams (Refer to above)

Mike Adams (Refer to above)

Nick Adams (Refer to above)

Tracy Adams (Refer to above)

Jared Alden unknown origin

Janie Anderson Grew up in Gerlach and graduated from Gerlach High School.

(Tom) **TA** and **Sherry Anderson** Tom was at one time a sheriff in town and Sherry was the school librarian. They had to leave when the United States Gypsum Corporation plant closed in 2011. Michelle and Janie Anderson were their children.

Herbert W. Armstrong Herbert W. Armstrong (1892–1986) founded the Radio Church of God in 1933 that later became the Worldwide Church of God. Armstrong was an early pioneer of radio and televangelism, proclaiming that he was preaching in a spiritual wilderness of religious confusion. In 1934, Armstrong began the publication of *The Plain Truth*. Armstrong started making prophetic claims asserting that Hitler and Mussolini were the prophesied Beast and False Prophet of the Book of Revelation who would deceive the nations for a short time just before the return of Jesus Christ.

B

George Barker DeWayne Williams's first cousin.

Jim Barker DeWayne Williams's uncle, on his mother's side.

Abram Barrie This references both Abram and Barrie Minnette. Barrie was a teacher in Gerlach; Abram is her son. Ralph, Barrie, Abram, and Dean Minnette — Ralph and Barrie still reside in Gerlach.

Drew Barrymore The actress was in Gerlach to do the movie *Far from Home* (1989).

Gary and **Suzie Beck** Suzie Beck worked at the Senior Center.

Cleo Benner Cleo was a real old-timer of the area who was Lois Ugalde's mother. DeWayne Williams mentions her in the nearly two-hour 1992 source video recording of Dooby Lane. "That was the first lady I ever fell in love with . . . her parents [were] making moonshine up in the ranch where I lived. He was a judge . . . well anyway, she was 18, 19, 20 or something like that, boy she was so beautiful and I fell in love with her, and she's never changed."

Jeff and **Ricka Benum** Jeff and Ricka Benum were friends of Ardyss (Ardie) and fans of Dooby's work.

George Bertoglio George Bertoglio was a cook at Bruno's Country Club; the stone honoring him had a slot machine carved into it.

Al, **Linda**, and **Jim Boegle** Dooby's daughter's deceased husband's family.

Dale Boegle Dale Boegle was DeWayne Williams's oldest daughter's husband; he later died of cancer. From the 1992 transcription: "I tell you this guy is over 54. And he used to be a champion bull rider when he was younger and he's been out of it for years and years and he broke his ankle. And so now all of a sudden he decides to go back in there 54 years old and tame those damn bulls. And he went down to California and made two rides—first time he got bucked off, next time he took second place and now he's heading for the gold."

John and **Mary Bogard** John and Mary Bogard, founders of the ceramic studio Planet X, adopted Travis Bogard. Mary later died of cancer and John married Rachel.

Travis Bogard (Refer to above)

Anna Bonilla The tablet PRETTY THINGS TO SEE IN GERLACH refers to women Dooby identified as attractive women. Anna Bonilla fit into this category.

Doug Brady Doug was a Washoe County sheriff from 1991 to 2013. Doug Brady was nicknamed "Rambo" for the number of DUI arrests he recorded in the Gerlach area.

Brent Carter Brennan and **Jacob Brennan** Both Brent and Jacob are grandchildren to the David and Gayle Carter family in Gerlach. These engraved tablets may have been added after DeWayne Williams's death.

Margie Broderick Margie was from Reno are served on the Washoe County School Board representing the Gerlach area.

Dan and **Robin Burgoyne** Robin is DeWayne's youngest daughter. She divorced Dan and is now Robin Collum.

Leo Buscaglia (1924–1998) American author and motivational speaker best known for his popular books including *Living, Loving and Learning* (1982), *Loving Each Other* (1984), *Born for Love* (1992), and *Leo Buscaglia's Love Cookbook* (1994).

President George Bush Given the timing of the tablet, this is most probably George Herbert Walker Bush (born June 12, 1924), an American politician who served as the 41st President of the United States (1989–93) and the 43rd Vice President of the United States (1981–89).

C

Linda Campbell Linda used to live in Empire and work at the United States Gypsum Corporation plant in Empire, Nevada.

Laszlo Cantos, Jr. unknown origin

Jerry Carlson unknown origin

[William] **Bill**, **Sherry**, and **Linda Carter** Bill and Sherry Carter were and have been longtime residents of Gerlach. Bill died in a freak accident in March 18, 2007. Sherry is the secretary at the Friends of Black Rock office. Linda is their daughter.

Crystal Carter Alumna of Gerlach High School (1983–1987).

Dave, **Gail**, and **Renee Carter** Dave and Gail Carter have been longtime residents of Gerlach. Crystal and Renee are their daughters.

Eileen Carter Eileen Carter is a longtime resident of Gerlach. Bill, David, and John are her children.

John and **Cindy Carter** John and Cindy now live in Eileen's home after she left Gerlach to live with a family member in California.

Linda Carter (2) Linda (Bill and Sherry's daughter) was a student at Gerlach High School and she graduated in 1989. Today, the school is called Gerlach K-12 Schools.

Jeanie Casey Jeanie was known for her ex-husband John Casey, a long-time Gerlach rancher who owned the Fly Ranch. Fly Geyser is located on the grounds of the Fly Ranch, which was sold to Todd Jaksick in 1998 and in 2016 to the Burning Man Project. Jeanie Casey's rock was at one time the biggest individual rock that Dooby put on the avenue, a testament to her standing as a member of the community.

Cheryl Cheryl was married to Larry Harbor, family friends of DeWayne Williams.

Chuck, **Brenda** and **Tina** unknown origin

Fred Chez Fred was a rancher in Gerlach.

Fred Jo Chez Fred and Jo Chez were married and lived in the mountains near Negro Creek (the creek was originally named on maps as "Nigger Creek" but was changed — refer to page 124, *Black Rock* by Peter Goin and Paul F. Starrs).

Edmond M. Ciel, Jr. unknown origin

Dave Clapper Dave Clapper was a recognized character who lived in Gerlach in the early 1990s.

Barbara Clark Barbara Clark worked at the United States Gypsum Corporation plant in Empire, Nevada.

President Bill Clinton William Jefferson "Bill" Clinton (born William Jefferson Blythe III; August 19, 1946) is an American politician who served as the 42nd President of the United States from 1993 to 2001. President Bill Clinton is married to Hillary Rodham Clinton.

Hil [broken tablet] **Rodham Clinton** (Refer to entry under Hilary [sic])

Tony Cochran unknown origin

Lum Coleman Lum Coleman was a Vietnam vet from Oakland, California, who was given a tour of Dooby Lane by Dan Deveny. Coleman carved his stone ONE OF THE WALKING DEAD and asked if it could be placed by the Vietnam Memorial display. He was wounded in Vietnam, lost consciousness, and awoke in a body bag among the dead.

Bud and **Barb Conley** Bud "buckaroo" and Barb Conley (Judy Conley's mother- and father-in-law) were longtime Gerlach residents. Bud was working as a cowboy at one of the ranches when he met his future wife, Barb. She graduated from Gerlach High School in 1947. Bud Conley supervised the quarry operations for the United States Gypsum Company in Empire and was the chairman of the Gerlach General Improvement District Board.

Tim Conley Judy Conley's son.

Torri Conley Torri Conley is Judy Conley's daughter. Both Tim (above) and Torri were students at Gerlach High School.

C. E. Coop, M.D. Charles Everett Koop, MD (1916–2013) was an American pediatric surgeon and public health administrator. He was a vice admiral in the Public Health Service Commissioned Corps and served as the 13th Surgeon General of the United States under President Ronald Reagan (1982–1989).

Norm Cormier Norm and his wife Shirley owned one of the bar/restaurants in Gerlach.

Bruno Courtney William Bruno Courtney is the oldest son of Lena Courtney (Bruno Selmi's daughter). He is considered a fine mechanic.

Cecil Courtney (2) There is a big Cecil and a little Cecil. Big Cecil is Lena (Skeekie) Courtney's husband; Little Cecil is their youngest son.

Brian Covey Brian Covey is a longtime resident of Gerlach.

Jeff Cox Jeff Cox worked for the United States Gypsum Corporation in Empire.

Bud Cribley Bud Cribley worked for the BLM and with fellow official Jeff McCosker provided Dooby with paperwork legitimizing his use of the public domain for his art project along a portion of what had been the old road to Gerlach. (Refer to Jeff McCosker.)

D

David This refers probably to David Green, who was principal of Gerlach High School (1977–1998) at the time that DeWayne's daughter was in school. David Green was Madge and Dell Green's son, married to Susie Green with daughter Becky.

Don, **Rita**, and **Donny Davis** Don, Rita, and Donny were longtime residents of Gerlach. Don and Rita have both passed away and their son Donny is in a group home in Reno.

Mary Desperban Mary Desperban was an old-timer who lived on Main Street in Gerlach. Patsy Stimac, listed alphabetically below, was her daughter.

Lisa Devall unknown origin

Dan Deveny (2) Dan was DeWayne Williams's right-hand man on Dooby Lane. He has the most knowledge of the avenue's history.

Derek Deville unknown origin

Bob Dixson Bob Dixson was a Vietnam vet who was memorialized by the stone I DONE MY PART. He worked around Gerlach from time to time.

Paula Dorr Paula Dorr, from 1992 transcription: "You can look at a person and say I don't like that guy, and turn around and a different guy says, hey, that's a good guy. So it's not what you're looking at, it's what you're seeing. Whatever you want to make." The stone: IT IS NOT WHAT YOU ARE LOOKING AT / IT IS WHAT YOU ARE SEEING / PAULA DORR.

Drew Douglas Drew and Skipper Douglas are married and are active members of the Gerlach community.

Skipper Douglas (Refer to above)

Vanessa Dunnican Vanessa Dunnican was a schoolteacher's daughter who graduated in 1996 from Gerlach High School.

Mary Duran Mary was Tony Duran's wife, although the context for this stone is unknown.

Bob Dylan Bob Dylan (born Robert Allen Zimmerman, May 24, 1941) is an American singer-songwriter, artist, and writer. He has been influential in popular music and culture for more than five decades. His celebrated work dates from the 1960s when his songs chronicled social unrest as early songs such as "Blowin' in the Wind" and "The Times They Are a-Changin" became anthems for the American civil rights and anti-war movements.

E

Burt Eckhardt Burt Eckhardt was an old-timer of the area and DeWayne Williams's neighbor.

May Edwards May Edwards was an emergency medical technician serving the greater Gerlach community. (Refer to May Timothy; Edwards was May's maiden surname.)

Elvis Elvis Aaron Presley (1935–1977) was an American musician and actor. Regarded as one of the most significant American cultural icons of the 20th century, Elvis is often referred to as the "King of Rock and Roll," or simply "The King." Dee Williams helped sculpt the rocks for the Elvis monument. Dee created Elvis's cape out of 1,200 aluminum can sections, tied together with fishing lure.

Al and **Vicki Enlow** Vicki Enlow is now Vicki Williams, having married DeWayne Williams's great-nephew Tim.

Lucille Evans Lucille Evans, now deceased, was married to Al Evans, with daughters Terry Vesey and Sherry Carter.

F

Jerry Falwell (2) Jerry Falwell Sr. (1933–2007) was an American evangelical Southern Baptist pastor, televangelist, and a controversial conservative political commentator. He was the founding pastor of the Thomas Road Baptist Church, a megachurch in Lynchburg, Virginia.

Richard Farnsworth Richard Farnsworth, now deceased, was a Vietnam vet who wanted a rock at the avenue's Vietnam memorial.

Geraldine Ferraro Geraldine A. Ferraro (1935–2011) worked as an assistant district attorney before being elected as a Democrat to the U.S. House of Representatives in 1978. She was the first woman to chair her party's 1984 platform committee and the first female vice presidential nominee, running with Walter Mondale. She later worked for the U.N. and with Hillary Clinton.

Edwin, **Barbara**, **Michelle**, **Daniel**, and **Edwin Ferris** Edwin Ferris worked on the railroad out of Gerlach. This is his family.

Tyler Flowers Tyler was a student at Gerlach High School. He was DeWayne Williams's great-great-nephew.

Pres. Jerry Ford Ret. Gerald Rudolph Ford Jr. (born Leslie Lynch King Jr., 1913–2006) served as the 38th President of the United States from 1974 to 1977. He was the 40th Vice President of the United States, serving from 1973 until President Richard Nixon's resignation in 1974. He was the first person appointed to the vice presidency under the terms of the 25th Amendment, following the resignation of Vice President Spiro Agnew on October 10, 1973. Becoming president upon Richard Nixon's departure on August 9, 1974, he was the first and to date the only person to have served as both Vice President and President of the United States without being elected to either office.

Logan Forster Logan and Shelby Forster were the children of the owner of Granite Propane. Both have grown and moved away, but Logan still delivers propane to the area.

Shelby Forster (Refer to above)

G

Joe Garcia Joe Garcia, a Yaqui (Indian) and now deceased, was at the time an elderly resident of Gerlach who lived next door to DeWayne Williams. His village in Mexico was besieged by smallpox when he was six years old, and Joe Garcia was one of only two survivors.

Bill Gladwill Bill Gladwill is the grandson of one of DeWayne's cousins.

Richard Dick Golden Dick Golden, neighbor of DeWayne, passed away on August 4, 2008.

Billy, **Karen**, and **Jillian Gooch** Bill was a young man when DeWayne Williams was around. Bob and Marion are his parents. Karen is Billy's wife, Jillian his daughter. Bob and Marion live in Gerlach now, right next door to Bill. Bill has been an emergency medical technician and fireman in the area for quite some time.

Bob Gooch (Refer to above) DeWayne Williams appreciated all the help that Bob Gooch provided for the community and citizens of Gerlach.

Marion Gooch (Refer to above) Marion and Bob Gooch were married.

Mikhail Gorbachev Mikhail Gorbachev was the first president of the Soviet Union, serving from 1990 to 1991. He was awarded the Nobel Peace Prize for his leadership role in ending the Cold War and promoting peaceful international relations.

Raisa Gorbachev Raisa Maximovna Gorbacheva (1932–1999) was the wife of Soviet leader Mikhail Gorbachev.

Anne Gordon unknown origin

Vice President Al Gore Albert Arnold "Al" Gore Jr. (born March 31, 1948) is an American politician and environmentalist who served as the 45th Vice President of the United States from 1993 to 2001 under President Bill Clinton. He was reelected Vice President in 1996. At the end of Clinton's second term, Gore was the Democratic Party's nominee for President in 2000. After leaving office, Gore remained prominent as an author and envi ronmental activist, whose work in climate change activism earned him jointly with the Intergovernmental Panel on Climate Change (IPCC) and the Nobel Peace Prize in 2007.

Billy Graham William Franklin "Billy" Graham Jr. (born November 7, 1918) is an American evangelical Christian, ordained as a Southern Baptist minister, who preached to a core constituency of middle-class, moderately conservative Protestants. He held large indoor and outdoor rallies; sermons were broadcast on radio and television.

Charlie Greear Charlie Greear was the resident sheriff during DeWayne Williams's work on Dooby Lane. Doug Brady (refer to above) and Charlie Greear were partners.

Becky Green Becky Green was David Green's daughter, Madge and Dell's granddaughter.

Dell Green Madge's husband. On January 10, 1940, he married his high school sweetheart and classmate, Madge Willardson of Redmond, Utah. He preceded Madge in death by just a brief two weeks on March 25, 2008.

Madge Green Madge Green was Dell's wife, and the postmaster at Empire. She worked as the postmaster for 23 years, until she retired in 1985. She died April 8, 2008. From the 1992 transcription: "And there is a very precious lady over there, boy, precious is a big word, you ever look it up in the dictionary? Man it covers a half a page telling about precious and that lady is precious. You know my wife is sick and she'd come down and brought her pies and she made some, she's a wonderful cook." The rock: WORKAHOLIC DELL GREEN/ A VERY PRECIOUS LOVELY LADY MADGE GREEN.

Rhonda Green David Green's daughter, Madge and Dell's granddaughter.

Beth Groendyk One of the schoolteachers at the Gerlach elementary school. She was married to Jim Watt and their daughter was Kimberly. The rock with Beth's name on it refers to the stone, ONE STEP FROM PERFECT.

Jola Guisasola Jola Guisasola (now Jola Mott) is the Gerlach postmaster.

Tricia Guisasola Tricia attended Gerlach High School from 1992 to 1994. She is Larry Guisasola's daughter. Larry owns Joe's Gerlach Club.

H

Al and **Kelli Hansen** Kelli Hansen lived within the Orient Farms area. Kelli was the daughter of Joan and Ted Grant, who operated a hay business in Hualapai Valley north of Gerlach. She and Al were husband and wife.

Taty Hansen unknown origin

Jason Hanson unknown origin

Kayra Hanson unknown origin

Tim Hanson unknown origin

Larry Harbor Larry Harbor was a family friend of DeWayne Williams. He died at 40 years old in the early 1980s. Cheryl Harbor was his wife.

John Harris John Harris was a cook at Bruno's Country Club and occasionally attended the Senior Citizen Center lunches. John would interrupt Dooby's stories, derailing Dooby's train of thought. This was frustrating, so Dooby's solution was to put some pressure on John Harris with the dedicated rock WHAT RIGHT DO WE HAVE TO KILL A POTATO / DIG OUT EYES / SKIN IT ALIVE / BOIL IT TO DEATH?

Joanne Hartman Joanne Hartman lived in Empire, and at the time she was the receptionist at the Gerlach medical clinic. The rock was TOUCHED BY THE MOON GLOW JOANNE HARTMAN. From 1992 transcription: ". . . See now there's a gal with a beautiful complexion. And so I wrote her out here [that she] was touched by the moon glow. And she always wears a dress opened down there. She has a beautiful complexion. And I said if she went out in the middle of the desert and took her dress off she'd probably glow like the moon's glow. Touched by the moon's glow."

Jan Hendershot Jan Hendershot was one of Dooby's daughter's friends who was married four times. The stone VARIETY IS THE SPICE OF LIFE referred to Jan. She married Jim Pav (refer to entry, below).

Eric Henjum Eric Henjum was the kindergarten teacher's child. He may have played with DeWayne's grandchild.

Jamie Henson unknown origin

Manny Hernandez Manny Hernandez died on June 17, 2015, but lived in Empire for quite some time. In 1979, he married Paulette (Meister) and both of them worked for the United States Gypsum Company, from which they eventually retired.

Dr. Herz James Rudolph Herz, M.D. (1915–2013). His successful solo orthopedic practice grew into the Reno Orthopedic Clinic, still the largest Orthopedic Surgery group in Nevada. Jim Herz loved the Black Rock Desert.

Hilary (sic) [Clinton] Hillary Diane Rodham Clinton (born October 26, 1947) is the Democratic Party's nominee for President of the United States in the 2016 election. She was the 67th U.S. Secretary of State from 2009 to 2013. From 2001 to 2009, Clinton served as a U.S. Senator from New York. She is the wife of the 42nd President of the United States, Bill Clinton, and was First Lady of the United States during his tenure from 1993 to 2001.

Jim Hoffman unknown origin

Mildred Holland unknown origin

Saddam Hussein Saddam Hussein Abd al-Majid al-Tikriti (1937–2006) was the fifth President of Iraq, serving in this capacity from July 1979 until April 2003. He was a leading member of the revolutionary Arab Socialist Ba'ath Party and, later, the Baghdad-based Ba'ath Party. Saddam Hussein played a key role in the 1968 coup (later referred to as the 17 July Revolution) that brought the party to power in Iraq. In 2003, a coalition led by the United States invaded Iraq to depose Saddam, in which U.S. President George W. Bush and British Prime Minister Tony Blair accused him of possessing weapons of mass destruction and having ties to al-Qaeda.

I

Bernice Iveson Bernice and Dave Iveson owned the Iveson ranch. Dave is DeWayne's cousin. Both have passed now.

Dave Iveson (Refer to above)

Jim and **Linda Iveson** Jim is DeWayne's cousin and Linda is his wife.

Nancy Iveson Nancy Iveson was married to Dave and Bernice's son. She was a wonderful teacher at Gerlach High School.

J

Jesse Jackson Reverend Jesse Louis Jackson Sr. (born Jesse Louis Burns; October 8, 1941) is an American civil rights activist, Baptist minister, and politician. He was a candidate for the Democratic presidential nomination in 1984 and 1988 and served as a proposed U.S. Senator for the District of Columbia from 1991 to 1997. He is the founder of the organizations that merged to form Rainbow/PUSH.

Michael Jackson Michael Joseph Jackson (1958–2009) was an American singer, songwriter, record producer, dancer, and actor. His contributions to music, dance and fashion, in concert with his publicized personal life, made him a global figure in popular culture for more than four decades.

The Jacksons: **Andrew**, **Andrea**, **Chuckie**, **Tillie**, and **Grover** The Jackson family still live on their ranch outside of Gerlach. They are brothers and sisters; Andrew Jackson was the father and is now deceased. The Jackson family is highly regarded and it is worthy to note that the children lived with their father until his death.

Gaylen and **Kathy James** Kathy James was one of Dooby's daughter's friends. She was married to Gaylen at the time.

Ray and **Ruby Janis** (2) Ray and Ruby were an elderly Paiute couple who lived on the side of the mountain near Highway 447. They would come to Gerlach to visit the local establishments. They passed away years ago.

Ardie Johns (2) DeWayne's oldest daughter, now Ardie Canon.

K

Kari unknown origin

Ron Kepler Ron Kepler is partner of the Reno Gerlach Stage Lines. Founded in 1992, Reno Gerlach Stage Lines is a small local and suburban transit company in Sparks, Nevada. His wife, Cathy Kepler, passed away February 8, 2010. From 1992 transcription: "This here is the most important man I could think of, brings our mail all the way over from Reno, you always go over expecting something. Or I do. What am I getting in the mail today. Maybe I got a great big check, maybe I won the sweepstakes, maybe I got a letter from God, saying hey man, let's meet somewhere. The most important man is the mailman." The rock: MOST IMPORTANT MAN/ RON KEPLER/ I HAUL THE MAIL.

David Koresh David Koresh (born Vernon Wayne Howell; 1959–1993) was the American leader of the Branch Davidians religious sect. The U.S. Bureau of Alcohol, Tobacco, Firearms and Explosives' agents conducted an investigation into illegal possession of firearms and explosives that resulted in the dramatic 1993 raid on the Branch Davidians compound in Waco, Texas. Four ATF agents and six Davidians were killed during the initial two-hour firefight. The subsequent siege by the FBI ended with the burning of the center, where Koresh and 79 others were found dead after the fire.

L

Donna Lacey Donna lived in Gerlach for a short period of time and ended up marrying DeWayne Williams's daughter Robin's first husband Doug Watt. They are still married and live in Florida.

Jerry Larson unknown origin

Bruce Lee Bruce Lee (1940–1973) was a revered martial

artist, actor, and filmmaker known for movies like *Fists of Fury* and *Enter the Dragon* and the technique Jeet Kune Do.

C Lockhart C Lockhart is as of this writing unidentified.

Huey Long Huey Pierce Long Jr. (1893–1935) was an American politician who served as the 40th Governor of Louisiana from 1928 to 1932 and as a member of the U.S. Senate from 1932 until his assassination in 1935. Huey Long was a Democrat and an outspoken populist who denounced the rich and the banks.

Lena Luccesi Lena arrived in Gerlach from Italy. She is responsible for encouraging Bruno Selmi (refer to entry, below) to move to the United States.

Jackie, **Cyd,** and **Kelly Lyles** Very close Williams family friends. The rock had Cyd's name misspelled as SID.

Terrell Lynn Terrell Lynn Thomas was a former resident who played for years with a band at the Miner's Club. He was a DJ at KFAT in the San Francisco Bay area. He played bass in Lacy J. Dalton's touring band and was a virtual encyclopedia of folk music.

M

Madge This is Madge Green (refer to entry, above). She and her husband built a home in Gerlach. She was the postmaster in Empire for many years. Her son David was the school principal for more than 20 years during the time DeWayne Williams lived in Gerlach.

Gabriella Marcionelli Gabriella was one of the many ladies appreciative of Dooby and his work. Dooby would naturally return the compliment in stone.

Annette Marshall The tablet PRETTY THINGS TO SEE IN GERLACH refers to women Dooby identified as attractive women.

Jennifer Dawn Martin Dooby identified Jennifer Dawn Martin as an attractive woman.

Jeff McCosker Jeff McCosker worked for the BLM and with fellow official Bud Cribley (refer to entry, above) provided Dooby with paperwork legitimizing the presence of his work on the avenue. (Dooby Lane was often called 'the avenue' by DeWayne and Dan.)

Ken and **Irene McCurdy** Ken and Irene lived in Empire; Ken was the Town Manager.

James Bruce McKnight This is Bev Osborn's oldest son. He was killed in Vietnam and his stone is at Dooby's Vietnam memorial.

Randy McKnight Randy is Bev Osborn's (of the Miner's Club) younger son and still lives in Gerlach. He is married to Risa, and their daughters are Shellie and Ranie.

Ranie McKnight Loraine (Ranie, Rani, or Rainy) and Shellie are Randy's daughters. They grew up in Gerlach.

Shellie McKnight Alumna of Gerlach High School (1989–1993).

Edwin Meese Edwin "Ed" Meese III (born December 2, 1931) is an American attorney, law professor, author, and member of the Republican Party who served in the Ronald Reagan Gubernatorial Administration (1967–1974), the Reagan Presidential Transition Team (1980), and the Reagan White House (1981–1985). He was the 75th Attorney General of the United States (1985–1988), a position from which he resigned while under investigation from a special prosecutor. DeWayne Williams placed this tablet on a desert packrat's nest.

Ivan Meyers Ivan and Norma Meyers were DeWayne Williams's neighbors. Norma ran the Senior Center for many years. Both have passed away. Their daughter now lives in their home in Gerlach.

Norma Meyers (2) From 1992 transcription: "If it wasn't for Norma there would be no palace down there for the seniors, for you and I to go to and get in arguments." The rock: SOLID AS A ROCK LITTLE MOTHER NORMA MEYERS.

Buddy Rocketman Michaelson The Aero-Pac Rocket Club asked that DeWayne Williams create a tablet for the group.

Ky Michaelson unknown origin

Mike Possibly Mike Minto (see Gary and Trudy Minto, below).

Abram Minnette Abram was Mary Minnette's grandson.

Mary Minnette (2) Mary is the matriarch of the Minnette family. At last report, she was in a nursing home. She is an old-time Gerlach resident. She was married to Chris Minnette. Ralph (below) is her son, Barry, her daughter-in-law, and Dea and Abram are her grandchildren.

Ralph Minnette (see Mary Minnette, above).

Richard Minor Richard Minor was a former Reno Justice of the Peace and Washoe District Court Judge from 1983 to 1984. Dooby memorialized Minor with HANG THEM HIGH BUT NOT BLOND LADIES.

Buddy Minto (see Gary and Trudy Minto, below).

Gary and **Trudy Minto** Trudy Minto, now deceased, was Judy Conley's sister. Trudy and Judy were DeWayne Williams's great-nieces. Gary grew up in Gerlach. Mike is his brother. Buddy and Russell are Gary and Trudy's children.

Russell Minto (see Gary and Trudy Minto, above).

Tom and Maureen Moore (1991) Tom and Maureen were friends of Don and Dinky Wardle (refer to entry, below). They visited often but never moved to or lived in Gerlach.

Cesar Moreno Cesar Moreno was born in 1972 and lives in Sparks, Nevada. He grew up in Gerlach and graduated from Gerlach High School in 1990.

Marie Morrissi The stone with Marie Morrissi's name came from a display originally placed on the avenue by Skipper Douglas. In that display, Marie was a "total friend" and her husband Drew was a "Hamms beer champion." The display was painted on cinder blocks and the first non-Dooby addition on the avenue. Dooby didn't remove it but instead duplicated each text on tablets using his hammer and chisel. He prefixed the display with a celebratory rock for Skipper and concluded the display with another rock following the "Hamms beer champion" with an engraved tablet, A LOT OF PP. Dooby was simply acknowledging that a beer champion might have to pee a lot. Dooby's sense of humor is revealed once again.

Lloyd Custer Mosley The Mosley family history is part of Gerlach's history. His middle name is not "Custer," but he was called that because of his looks.

Ray, **Linda**, **Karla**, and **Mike Mosley** Ray Mosley is Lloyd's brother and still lives in Gerlach. Linda has passed. Karla and Mike are his children.

Ashley Mott (2) Possibly Ashly Mott, alumnus of Gerlach High School (2000–2004).

Jola Mott Jola Guisasola married Danny Mott. Ashley is her daughter. Jola is the granddaughter of Ann Selmi, Joe's Gerlach Club.

Dennis Murphy Dennis and Sharin lived in Gerlach for a period of time. Dennis worked for the county.

Sharin Murphy (Refer to above)

N

Nancy This rock refers to either Nancy Iveson (refer to entry under Iveson) or Nancy Reagan, of "Just Say No" fame.

Art and **Roy Nish** Roy Nish (short for Nishiguchi) and his brother Art both have rocks on the avenue. Art and Roy came to Nevada along with their parents and five sisters when their father transferred from Utah with the Union

Pacific Railroad. At the onset of WWII, they were given 24 hours to vacate railroad property. Art and DeWayne Williams grew up together in Gerlach and were very close friends their entire adult life. Art, who died January 18, 2010, joined the army about the same time DeWayne Williams joined the Marine Corps. Art is in the Reno-Sparks Bowling Hall of Fame. The oldest daughter in the Nishiguchi family, Mary Chadwell, who died at 98 years old in 2012, was a painter of miniatures. Art was the only one who changed his last name to Nish, in part because people had such a hard time pronouncing Nishiguchi.

Oliver North Oliver North (born October 7, 1943) was a former deputy-director of the National Security Council. He was implicated in the Iran-Contra affair and forced to resign. He was convicted of three charges, which were overturned in 1990.

Rhonda Nuttle Rhonda Nuttle is Bud and Barbara Conley's daughter and Judy Conley's sister-in-law.

O

Mary Obert Beth Obert was the custodian of Gerlach High School for many years. Mary Obert was her daughter and, by Dooby's account, very attractive.

Bev and **Arley Osborn** Bev and Arley were the owners of the Miner's Club in downtown Gerlach. Arley passed away on January 8, 1995; Bev owns the Miner's Club.

P

Donna Pardee Donna Pardee married Dooby's former son-in-law Doug Watt after he and Dooby's daughter divorced. The stone is YANKEE'S FIRST BAT GIRL.

Garrett Paschall Garrett Paschall is Ray and Betty's son and a member of the Gerlach community.

Ray and **Betty Paschall** Ray died May 4, 1994, but Betty still lives in Gerlach. They were DeWayne Williams's neighbors.

Jim Pav Jim Pav was married to Jan Hendershot (refer to entry, above), which was her fourth marriage.

Gene and **Anita Pfaff** Both are old-timers of Gerlach, both deceased. Eugene died on April 20, 2006.

Alberta Phillips Alberta Phillips, now deceased, was from Gerlach. Her children are Barbara, Bernice, Jack, and Ralph. Barbara married Bud Conley, Bernice married Dave Iveson, Ralph married Evelyn, and Jack married Violet.

Evelyn Phillips (Refer to above)

Jess Phillips Jess Phillips had no relation to Evelyn. Jess worked on the railroad.

Sam Philpott Sam Philpott worked for Bruno Selmi (refer to entry, below).

Joe Pinedo Joe Pinedo from Jalisco, Mexico, was the owner of the Jalisco Club, which is currently the site of the Friends of Black Rock-High Rock.

Vickie Poetstra unknown origin

Bob Price unknown origin

Kelly Price unknown origin

Q

Elisse Quinn Elisse Quinn is the daughter of a teacher at Gerlach High School.

Louise Quintera Louise (Romo) Quintera was a friend of DeWayne's daughter Robin, and they graduated together from Gerlach High School in 1980.

R

Ralph Ralph Phillips, an old cowboy who was Barbara Conley's and Bernice Iveson's brother. His wife's name was Evelyn and his mother was Alberta (refer to Alberta Phillips, above).

Susan Rios (2) Susan Rios is the daughter of Tom and Diana Rios and first cousin to DeWayne Williams's daughter Robin's oldest son, Dillon Watt.

Tomcat and **Diana Rios** Tom "Tomcat" and Diana have divorced. Diana still lives in Gerlach.

Scott Robinson unknown origin

Stuart, **Marge**, **Justine**, and **Sandy Robinson** Stuart and his family have lived in Gerlach many years. Stuart still cowboys and he is in his eighties. The children have moved, and his wife, Marjorie Ann, died January 2, 2007.

Louise Romo (Refer to Louise Quintera, above)

Irene and **Arcadio Ruvaleaba** Irene worked at the elementary school and Arcadio is her husband.

S

Sparky Sallsbury Sparky Sallsbury's stone was SURE FILLS OUT A SHIRT.

Sandy and **Nettie** Sandy and Nettie were friends who met in Gerlach to go camping in the Black Rock. Dan Deveny introduced them to Dooby, who gave them a tour of the avenue. Two weeks later, Sandy returned to Gerlach to see Dan and she was able to see the rock that Dooby had engraved BOY HOWDY. Dan married Sandy a couple years later, and that was more than 20 years ago, and they are still married.

Ace Sauers Ace Sauers is associated with the stone THE LOST WEEKEND LIVES HERE. Ace did odd jobs for Helen Thrasher (refer to entry, below). He died in the hospital from cirrhosis of the liver.

Sunny Schatz Sunny Schatz is now Sunny DeForest. Sunny still resides in the area. She was the human resources person at the United States Gypsum Corporation plant in Empire.

Viola Seeley Viola (Tracey) Seeley was DeWayne Williams's daughter Robin's school friend.

Joe Selmi Joe Selmi, now deceased, was Bruno's brother and the owner of Joe's Gerlach Club. Joe was married to Annie Selmi, Jola Mott's grandmother.

King Bruno Selmi DeWayne Williams added the title of "King" honoring Bruno Selmi, owner of Bruno's Country Club. "King" Bruno built himself into a Gerlach landmark. Bruno emigrated with his younger brother Joe from northern Italy to Nevada shortly after World War II. Bruno worked at the gypsum mine in nearby Empire before opening his first Gerlach bar in 1950. The restaurant opened in 1972 but burned down in 1982.

Fred Shoenfeldt Fred Shoenfeldt was married to DeWayne Williams's niece Marge. Judy Conley is their daughter.

Gary Snyder Coauthor of this book (refer to author section, page 117).

Sophia and **Audry** Dooby and Dan found Sophia and Audry sleeping on Dooby Lane. They had come up to the Black Rock for a few days in the desert. Their memorialized stone was BEAUTY AND LIGHT.

Bob and **Edna Spoo** Bob and Edna Spoo ranched in the area for a long time and raised their children Bill and Jim in Gerlach. Bill is still around Gerlach (as of this writing). Bill handled Fly Ranch's visitor inquires. Jim became the mayor of Sparks, Nevada, and a Sparks Municipal Judge.

Bill Stapleton Bill Stapleton, now deceased, was often one of the first people visitors and those passing through Gerlach would meet. He operated the gas station for Bruno.

Mike Stewart Mike Stewart owned Empire Farms and at one time Orient Farms. He still visits Gerlach when he can.

Chrissy Stimac Patsy Stimac's daughter (refer to entry for Patsy Stimac, below).

Lisa Stimac Patsy Stimac's daughter.

Patsy Stimac (2) Patsy Stimac was Mary Desperban's daughter (refer to entry above). Patsy married a school principal named Stimac. Chrissy, Lisa, and Paul are her children. Patsy raised her children by herself in Gerlach.

Paul Stimac Patsy Stimac's son.

Joe Stromer "Opal Joe" is an old-timer and miner who lives somewhere in the mountains northwest of Gerlach.

Sue unknown origin

Ruth Swafford Ruth and her husband Frank lived behind the grocery store in Empire. Her husband worked for the United States Gypsum Corporation plant. From 1992 transcription: ". . . that Ruth, man, she's one of the best cooks." The stone is A GREAT COOK. Ruth cooked at the Senior Center.

Jim Swaggart Jimmy Lee Swaggart (born March 15, 1935) is an American Christian music singer, Pentecostal pastor, author, and televangelist. His 1980s radio and television broadcasts were transmitted to over 3,000 stations and cable systems each week. Sexual scandals in the late 1980s and early 1990s resulted in his defrocking by the Assemblies of God. As a result, Swaggart's ministry became non-affiliated, non-denominational, and significantly smaller than it was in the ministry's pre-scandal years.

Bill and **Lola Sweet** Bill and Lola owned the old hotel on Main Street in Gerlach. Both have passed away. Bill worked on the county crew and Lola drove the school bus and cooked for years at Gerlach High School.

T

Jim and **Lindy Taylor** Dooby's family friends.

Chris Thompson Chris Thompson, now deceased, was a cowboy at the time. He grew up in Empire.

Helen Thrasher (1898–2001) Helen and her husband were among the earliest residents of Gerlach. She was the postmaster for 45 years. When DeWayne Williams needed an affidavit affirming his birth, Helen Thrasher provided sworn testimony on his behalf. Helen and her husband ran the general mercantile store in Gerlach and brought the initial electrical power to Gerlach. She would shut the generator off at midnight, ending her husband's card playing.

May Timothy (Refer to May Edwards, above).

Tipper (Gore) Mary Elizabeth "Tipper" Gore (born August 19, 1948) is an author, photographer, and social issues advocate who was Second Lady of the United States from 1993 to 2001. She is the wife of Al Gore, the 45th Vice President of the United States, from whom she is currently separated.

Viola Tracey Viola was the daughter of Gracie Tracey, an old-timer in Gerlach.

Gary Trosper unknown origin

Joel Turnbow Joel is Jola Mott's son. He was Joe Selmi's grandson.

Rory Paul Tyler At first, DeWayne Williams used a hammer and chisel to etch the rocks, but the effort required had taken its toll and he stopped working with the stones. Rory Paul Tyler had been working on a project in Reno that involved carving rocks and felt that his employer might be willing to make a contribution to the arts. The next weekend, Rory brought an electrical grinder with a diamond blade and presented it to Dooby. It took a few days for Dooby to realize that this would enable him to continue his work, albeit with a straighter block-style. At the same time, Dooby discovered a trove of suitable rocks in Parsnip canyon (wash) so he continued scribing on the stones. More than half the rocks were made using the diamond-bladed tool.

S. Tyler I LOVE MY CRITICS refers to S. Tyler's description of Dooby Lane as "corn."

U

Connie Ugalde Connie Ugalde was a waitress at the Jalisco Club, which was the last bar on Main Street. Connie was Joe Pineda's step-granddaughter. She married Mitch Ugalde, and Michael (below) is their son.

Joe Ugalde Joe was an old-timer from Gerlach who owned the propane company. Joe, his wife Lois and children Mike, Mitch, and Julie, and grandson Michael represent a long lineage in the greater Gerlach community.

Michael Ugalde (Refer to above)

Mike Ugalde (Refer to above)

V

Kippen Vesey Kippen Vesey grew up and went to school in Gerlach. The rock associated with Kippen Vesey is AND POETRY IS MY GAME. She is the granddaughter of Al and Lucille Evans, daughter of Terry Vesey.

Ben Vines unknown origin

W

David Wardle Possibly related to Owen and Carman Wardle.

Donald and **Dinky Wardle** Don Wardle was the maintenance man for the General Improvement District and an elected official of the District from 1997 to 2001. He and his wife Dinky are now deceased. The Gerlach General Improvement District provides water, disposal, and sewer services to the residents of the community. The office is located within the Gerlach Community Center.

Owen and **Carman Wardle** Owen, Don Wardle's uncle, has passed away, but his widow Carman still resides in Gerlach.

Big Jim and **Lois Watt** Jim Watt, now deceased, was an old-timer from Gerlach. Lois was his second wife. David is his grandson. Doug Watt was his son, once married to Robin (DeWayne's daughter). Dillon is Robin and Doug's son and DeWayne's grandson.

David Watt Alumnus of Gerlach High School (2007–2011).

Dillon Watt (2) DeWayne Williams's daughter Robin's son.

Mr. Dillon Dewayne Watt Dillon (Robin's son) often stayed with his grandparents DeWayne and Beth Williams.

Doug Watt (2) Doug Watt was a central person in DeWayne Williams's life.

Kimberley Watt Kimberley is Jim and Beth Watt's daughter.

Robin Watt Robin Williams through her first marriage became Robin Watt.

Cedric and **Evelyn Weeks** Cedric and Evelyn Weeks were an elderly couple who lived in Empire. As of this writing, Evelyn lives in Fernley.

Amy Weldon Amy Weldon was a student at Gerlach Elementary School. She graduated in 1995.

Cliff Weldon Clifford Weldon, Amy's father (above), an emergency medical technician at the time, was very important to the Gerlach community. He was a member of the Volunteer Gerlach Fire Department and worked for the United States Gypsum Company in Empire.

Floyd, **Pattie**, **Richard**, and **Jason Welles** Dooby's friends.

Wendy (1994) unknown origin

Whitey LOST WEEKEND LIVES HERE refers to Whitey, who worked at Bruno's gas station for many years.

Jackie Widel The rock associated with Jackie Widel was AN ORIGINAL. (Refer to the Skipper Douglas series, above.)

Beth Williams DeWayne Williams's wife. 1992 transcription: "That rock there, I'll tell you something, [BEST IN THE WEST BETH WILLIAMS] that's my wife . . . I put that rock there and every day I come out it was petrified with bird poop, they sit on there and shit all the way down that rock."

Bub, **Vicki**, and **Tanya Williams** Bub was DeWayne Williams's nephew (DeWayne's brother Clifford's son), Vicki was Bub's wife, and Tanya was Bub and Vicki's daughter.

Buster and **Elsie Williams** Buster was DeWayne's nephew (brother Harry's son) and Elsie is Buster's wife.

Clifford Williams DeWayne Williams's brother.

Dawson Williams Dee (DeWayne Williams's son) and wife Suelynn's son. (DeWayne Williams's grandson.) From 1992 transcription: "I got a grandson, that's going be a star quarterback. Man he's taken all kinds of trophies doing all kind of things in Montana. And they say he's going to be another Joe Montana."

DeWayne Williams (Refer to "The Guru of Dooby Lane," page 81).

DeWayne Williams Jr. DeWayne Williams's son, known as "Dee." He was involved in constructing many of the stone structures and Elvis's cape on the avenue.

Leonard Williams DeWayne Williams's nephew (brother Edward's son).

Philly Williams Philly Williams was an elderly lady who lived close to DeWayne Williams but there is not a family relation. Philly was Anita Phaff's sister (refer to entry, above). They were Basque and by all accounts lovely people.

Rani Williams DeWayne Williams's granddaughter.

Regan Williams DeWayne Williams's grandson.

Robin Williams (2) DeWayne Williams's youngest daughter.

Suelynn Williams DeWayne Williams's daughter-in-law (Dee's wife).

Tom Williams (2) DeWayne Williams's nephew (brother Cliff's son).

Tom, **Ginny**, and **Wes Williams** DeWayne Williams's nephew, his wife, and son. Tom and Wes live in Fallon.

Vicki Williams Vicki, alumna of Gerlach High School (1975–1979), is married to DeWayne Williams's great-nephew, Tim.

Betty Winebarger unknown origin

Hillary Winebarger unknown origin

Oprah Winfrey Billionaire Oprah Winfrey is best known for hosting her own internationally popular talk show from 1986 to 2011. She is also an actress, philanthropist, publisher, and producer.

Norma Worley Norma Worley was reportedly a student at Gerlach High School, although she is not listed among the alumni.

Jane Wyman Jane Wyman (1917–2007) was an Academy Award–winning American screen actress who was also Ronald Reagan's first wife.

Z

Joe, **Esther**, **Greg**, and **Christy Zabalas** unknown origin

Ken Zacharias Ken Zacharias was a physician's assistant in Gerlach. As of this writing, he is a physician's assistant in Yerington, Nevada. The stone tablet is ROCKIN DOC. Ken played a little electric guitar with great enthusiasm. He was a very fine diagnostician.

A Conversation

BETWEEN PETER GOIN
AND GARY SNYDER

This is a conversation between Peter Goin and Gary Snyder that occurred on the 7th of July 2016. The text of the conversation is condensed for relevance. In a few cases, explanatory text was added.

PG: PETER GOIN
GS: GARY SNYDER

PG: The order of the stone tablets is from the southwestern entrance to Dooby Lane to the northeastern exit before the paved highway. The photographs are in order of walking the avenue; the sequence was established spring 2016. The order of the tablets has somewhat changed over the years in part because of the microbursts that have washed away some of the stones. One tablet that makes me laugh is the Bob Dylan lyric "A Hard Rain's A-Gonna Fall" that washed away. I found it down the road, half buried in sand. My team and I keep spending time trying to find missing stones—people have stolen some, taking them, moving them; it's quite the kinetic avenue.

GS: So you have a complete sequence of photographs and then we would go into the complete sequence of actual writings?

PG: No, and the reason for that is because there are too many. We have the photographs in sequential order, your field notes, and then the names, which are in alphabetical order, so that people can easily look up their name.

GS: So that was one of my questions—is anybody going to object about having their name up there?

PG: Their name on the avenue is a compliment, and that's the spirit in which we've photographed, and catalogued everything. I have spoken with a few people and from what I've heard, most everybody is pleased that I am creating the Dooby Lane archive for public preservation. Of course, I'm really trying to dance a little bit around some of the life changes that people have experienced, you know, married this person, divorced that person, married someone else. I just want to be accurate without judgments. But so far, I've not had a single person say, "Don't do this." Most people say: "Oh! This is great and you need to talk to this person or that person."

GS: Oh, you know that is really good, because if you did this on the East Coast, people would be not supportive.

PG: When I go into the Black Rock, it's a tableau of fascination that I try to convey in my photography. As a poet, how do you approach a place like the Black Rock and the discovery of the avenue?

GS: I think of it as part of the phenomena of the surface of the earth and the way it seems to shape itself according to its own conditions, and I'm fascinated by what the conditions are that make such a place possible. Where they are in the surface of planet Earth, right now. Did you see that movie last year, the big action movie called *The Fury Road*?

GS: It's interesting for people like ourselves who take interest in landscape, in that much of it was filmed in the Namibian Desert, and I looked at that when the film was playing, and I said, "I don't know where that is." I was right; I looked it up later and found the Namib, the combination of big flat spaces and amazing rock formations.

PG: One of the elements of the Burning Man festival is that they write about or talk about this landscape as a tabula rasa, and I don't see it as a blank slate.

GS: Oh, well, a blank slate is just a thing to write on.

PG: Well, exactly. And while the participants are doing their own "writing" in the landscape, I see a landscape that is full of very unique and spectacular bio-communities. When I look at the Black Rock, I often talk about water evolving into light—the movement of light across the surface reminds me of the rhythms of tidal water.

GS: Oh, that's interesting . . . that is accurate to your perception.

PG: And you can see evidence of water everywhere, in the ancient shorelines and in the shells and in the kind of pre-historical artifacts, and in the hardscrabble nature of the terrain. The Black Rock region is phenomenal because you can see the curvature of the earth across the playa.

GS: I don't know if I ever told you, I had Wendell Berry out there with me one time, and we were sitting in little folding chairs having a glass of bourbon and the new moon was just setting and he was looking all around, and he said, "Gary, I don't think there'll be much farming here."

PG: Artists have a tremendous grasp of the obvious.

GS: That's only one kind of a desert and you don't get one that is all flat like this that easily. But that's part of the Lake Lahontan phenomenon. The Black Rock has been totally full and totally empty 27 times, I have read.

GS: I had to control myself to not talk about all that, when I was trying to write about the Dooby Lane.

PG: When I think about not just listening but inscribing in my own way, it's about imagining the resonance of words. When you experienced Dooby Lane, did you think about the sequence of the tablets as a poetic rhythm?

GS: I recorded Dooby Lane as it was in 1988, and I couldn't go back and take notes on what was further apart and what was closer together, so I was just trying to get it down as best as I could, the way I saw it the first time.

PG: I believe that your field notes are one of the earliest chronicles of the avenue. There is something immutable about stone carvings that imply immortality, but they have been moved or washed away, or added or subtracted, such that the avenue almost feels like it has a life of its own.

GS: Well, you know, historical scholarship in India and also in China in the last 20 years has really gone a lot into the study

Acknowledgments

Dooby Lane is within Black Rock country, northern Nevada. To those who travel the byways of this desert and range outback, driving through the alternative universe titled Guru Road is just part of the experience. While on the avenue, time slows and sometimes walking is faster, even in a summer's midday sun, as there's always a phrase that delights or a quote that provokes. My research team and I have made every effort to provide accurate information, but this is an ongoing project that has a life of its own.

While memory fades, and stories evolve, and the stones move, this book memorializes DeWayne Williams's creation, and his family deserves special mention for their help and generosity. This includes son DeWayne "Dee" Williams Jr. and daughters Ardyss Johns and Robin Collums, and Judy Conley, DeWayne's niece. Dan Deveny, DeWayne Williams's right-hand man, was there during most of the tablet days and knows nearly all the stories. During a long day's walk from one end of Dooby Lane to the other, Dan narrated the stones, telling stories that have been recorded by Scott Hinton and transcribed by my research assistants Shelby McAuliffe and Mychelle Vincent. These documents will reside with the rest of the visual and textual materials as a collection available for public use and review.

Scott Hinton, Coordinator of Photography Research, Department of Art, University of Nevada, Reno, made four photographs in the book and provided critical review of the stone tablets' sequence along the avenue.

My photographic research team consists of Scott and numerous student research assistants including but not limited to Charlie Briscoe and Danielle Smith, who graduated in May 2016. The research assistants worked on image cleaning, rock locations, and developing searchable word documents.

Stephen Davis, long-standing friend and companion, transcribed the first draft of names from the rocks onto paper. Michael Myers, Executive Director, The Friends of Black Rock-High Rock, is stewarding with a small legion of volunteers numerous projects to restore Dooby Lane. Margie Reynolds and Christina Preston shared information and their abiding interests in Gerlach and Dooby Lane.

The photographs and documents involved in the production of this book will join the records of other projects in the *Peter Goin Collection* in Special Collections, University of Nevada, Reno Libraries. Christina Spielvogel provided her photographs of Dooby Lane for inclusion in the *Peter Goin Collection*. Katrina Windon, photograph archivist, has been an essential team member in assisting with facilitating the *Peter Goin Collection*.

Finally, and simply, this book is about the love of poetry, in whatever form, and for that, I owe my friend Gary Snyder special thanks with deep appreciation of the poetry within us.

And may our memories of those no longer with us, including Chelsea Miller Goin who died at the exact time the accordion-fold book was assembled, and Carole Koda, who was with Gary in 1988 along the avenue, reflect the richness of the place we call Black Rock.

Peter Goin

About the Authors

PETER GOIN has spent the majority of his life in the great American outback that includes the Basin and Range country of northern Nevada. He is the author of books exploring paradigms of place, including *Tracing the Line: A Photographic Survey of the Mexican-American Border*; *Nuclear Landscapes*; *Stopping Time: A Rephotographic Survey of Lake Tahoe*; *Nevada Rock Art*; and *Humanature*. His recent book with Lucy Lippard, *Time and Time Again: History, Rephotography, and Preservation in the Chaco World*, explores the mysteries of time and identity in ancestral architecture.

Goin's photographs have been exhibited in more than fifty museums nationally and internationally, and he is the recipient of multiple awards, from the National Endowment for the Arts to Nevada Governor's Millennium Award for Excellence in the Arts.

Writer, bioregionalist, and scholar GARY SNYDER walked miles of trails and drove hundreds of miles of dirt roads in the Great Basin with his expert partner Carole Koda. They stumbled onto the Dooby Lane installation while searching for a rumored spring and campsite. Two lucky finds.

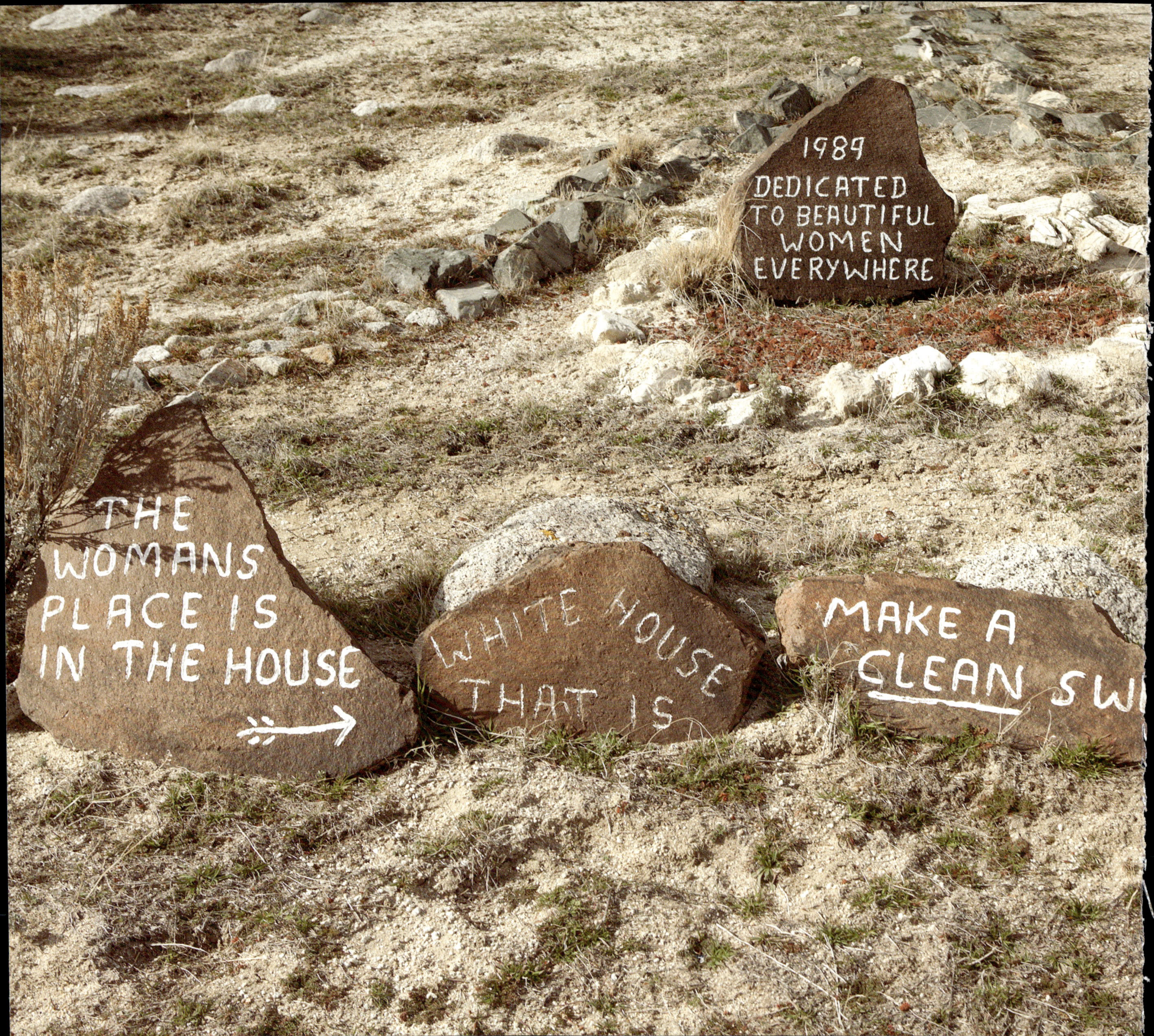
1989
DEDICATED
TO BEAUTIFUL
WOMEN
EVERYWHERE
THE
WOMANS
PLACE IS
IN THE HOUSE
WHITE HOUSE
THAT IS
MAKE A
CLEAN